Close to the Heart

Close to the Heart

A GUIDE TO PERSONAL PRAYER

Margaret Silf

Loyola Press

Chicago

Loyola Press

3441 North Ashland Avenue
Chicago, Illinois 60657

© 1999 by Margaret Silf
All rights reserved

Unless otherwise noted, all Scripture quotations are from the New Jerusalem Bible © 1985 by Darton Longman & Todd, Ltd., and Doubleday, a division of Bantam Doubleday Dell, Inc. Reprinted by permission.

Scripture quotations marked KJV are from the *Holy Bible,* King James Version.

Interior design by Leonard Telesca

Library of Congress Cataloging-in-Publication Data

Silf, Margaret.
    Close to the heart : a guide to personal prayer / Margaret Silf.
      p. cm.
    ISBN 0-8294-1452-5
    1. Prayer—Christianity. I. Title.
    BV210.2.S53 2000
    248.3'2—dc21   99-16816
                                         CIP

Printed in the United States of America
99 00 01 02 03 / 10 9 8 7 6 5 4 3 2 1

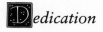

Dedication

Ad majorem dei gloriam

"How good Yahweh is —
only taste and see!"
　　　　　　— PSALM 34:8 JB

Contents

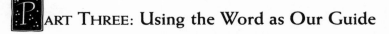

PART FOUR: Stumbling Blocks and Stepping Stones

Hearing God's Heartbeat

———

✳

It seems to be a fact of life: Everyone who ever thinks about "prayer" or tries to pray feels that everyone else can do it much more effectively. Perhaps we have dismissed as irrelevant our childhood "saying of prayers" and are unsure of how to find any more personal approach to God. Perhaps we feel that prayer is a secret, inaccessible space in the center of our hearts. We have some sense that God himself is dwelling in that place, but we have no idea of how to get there or of what to do if we could.

If anyone were to ask you to speak about your prayer life, you might run a mile in panic. *There's nothing to tell,* you might think. The space in your heart, where you feel God should be, may feel empty and deserted. Or it may feel dark and frightening. You might be afraid to reveal it to another, because it would make you so vulnerable and expose things in your depths that you would rather not bring into the daylight. Both of these very understandable and normal reactions have their roots in fear. We are afraid of facing, at the heart of ourselves, what may turn out to be "nothing" or something too dark to contemplate.

Suppose, however, that we could go back, at least in our imagination, to the Garden of Eden and notice how things were in the beginning. When I do this myself, I notice three things in particular that encourage me to take the risk of personal prayer:

- Before anything ever went wrong in the scheme of things, God looked at his creation and said that it was good.

- God walked daily through the paths of paradise with his created beings. Being on intimate terms, Creator and creature engaged in heart-to-heart conversations as a matter of course.

- It was fear that spoiled all this. For Adam and Eve, a fear of their inner darkness, their vulnerability, and their nakedness prevented this everyday intimacy with God.

Fear, then, puts a stop to our natural communion with God. Does it have to be a full stop? If God is dwelling in our innermost hearts, as Scripture affirms, how might we approach this sacred center of our existence? How might we come close to the heart of ourselves, there to discover the source and the destination of our being, in God, through prayer?

From experience I see that two things have happened, in my personal life and in the life of all creation, to block the communication with God that we call prayer:

- Fear has seduced me into putting up barricades around my heart, to keep a hostile world at bay. Inevitably, however, these same barricades have also kept me out of my innermost self and prevented my meeting there with God.

- Because I have fenced my heart in this way, I have quite literally lost my way. I am no longer on easy terms with God or with my own heart. I am no longer familiar with the paths to my own center. Even if I could find them, they would be overgrown with thorns and brambles and I would be afraid to walk along them.

The purpose of this book is:

- to dispel fears that keep us at a distance from the heart of our being, where God is, and to restore our confidence that God will welcome our approach and is already coming to meet us and assure us that he longs to reestablish that first communion with us;

• to open up pathways we may have lost (or may never have realized were there), to reveal specific ways of reaching into our hearts here and now, in the midst of our everyday living.

Not that prayer will lead us to a world of certainties, but it will give us ways of *being* in our uncertainty. This isn't a book for spiritual experts. It is a guide for the lost children of Eden, who know that they *don't* know but have enough trust to take the first step of opening their hearts to God in prayer and see where it leads them. I am taking these steps, these first steps, myself, and I expect still to be taking first steps on the day I die. I invite you to discover your own steps and let God build up your confidence, gradually and steadily, that this, truly, is a path that can be trusted.

Nor is this a book for "religious" people, except in that all of us are religious, because we are energized by God. If prayer is meaningful at all, it is meaningful for everyone, and it is to be discovered in the places where we live out our lives, not in some special "holy" (and ultimately unreal) place, to which we feel we have no access.

A Prayer Story

One year a friend decided to set aside Advent as a time for deeper personal prayer. But she found that her small daughter had other ideas. The child had set her heart on a particular soft toy, her only Christmas wish. The mother searched the toy shops in vain and ultimately decided that she would have to knit the toy herself.

And so the cherished prayer time seemed to be short-circuited as Christmas approached; the details of the knitting project took over. Barely knowing where to start, she gathered all colors of wool yarn scraps from around the house and from friends and relatives. Her search was exhaustive and exhausting. And then, as her imagination clicked as fast as her needles, she desperately hoped that the work of her hands would meet with her daughter's approval. Prayer seemed almost lost in an overloaded schedule in the service of her family. She tried to search for meaning in the daily work and hoped that God would accept the results.

On Christmas morning my friend knew her efforts had been fruitful. For days her daughter showed her new toy to everyone she met, with the proud and joyful introduction, "This is my Christmas present and my mommy knitted him herself!" The toy meant so much more to her than any machine-made equivalent the shops might have stocked.

"Mom" told me this story, full of regret for the prayer she had failed to make during Advent. But what I heard wasn't her regret, but God's delight over all she had discovered of God, of love, and of life during these weeks of preparation celebrating the life of another Child. This mother had gathered the scraps of her experience into her living prayer during that time, just as surely as she had gathered the scraps of wool for her daughter's toy. There was no doubt in my mind that God was sharing the story with the angels and saints, with the proud words: "This is prayer, and she knitted it herself!" Surely God rejoiced more over that homemade Advent prayer than over the formal retreat my friend never made!

There is more prayer in the scrap yards of our hearts than we imagine. If we look for signs in the heavens, we may easily overlook God's footprints in the sidewalk. The true vine is on the greengrocer's shelf. The pearl of great price lies hidden in the cracks of our city sidewalks. And the salt of the earth is what we sprinkle on our own potatoes.

Overview of This Book

Through this book I hope to help you explore some ways of becoming more aware of "God's footprints in the sidewalk"; if we follow them, they will lead us close to the heart of our own being and that of all creation. The book is divided into four sections.

Part 1, "Entering Prayer," looks at some guiding principles for a life of personal prayer: the discovery of God's life-generating presence within our own hearts and experience; the call to stillness; the positive power of our own desires; and the art of living reflectively, so that what we discover in the stillness of heart—called prayer— can permeate and invigorate our daily lives and routines.

Part 2, "Learning to Focus," gives a number of particular and specific suggestions for personal prayer. Each approach brings your everyday experience into the light of God's presence. Try these suggestions and see whether they bring any new light into your experience.

Part 3, "Using the Word as Our Guide," explores ways of praying with Scripture—ways in which God's Word, in its many forms, can be the gateway through which you enter into prayer.

Part 4, "Stumbling Blocks and Stepping Stones," offers a few thoughts on overcoming some difficulties and making use of some opportunities in the journey into prayer. I also suggest how you can make prayer become a way of life.

Short chapters within each part explore one approach to personal prayer. Each chapter also includes suggestions for exercises ("Taking It Further").

Some of these ways of prayer may appeal to you more than others. I suggest that you begin by reflecting on the foundations suggested in part 1. Then explore the various possibilities set out in the remainder of the book. Take and use anything you find helpful, and leave the rest. Remember that there are infinite ways of praying. No one way is ever the right way or the only way. What is right for you is what draws you closer to God and to your truest self, at this particular time and place in your journey. The approaches suggested here are merely the ones I have found helpful in my own search for God. I make no apology for the many omissions, because I can share only what I have experienced personally.

If you stand still and place a finger on your pulse point, you become aware of your heartbeat. The throbbing of your pulse, easily discernible on the outer edges of your being, is actually a manifestation of the life-giving energy constantly generated by your heart and circulating through your entire body.

In the same way we can stand still on the outer edges of our daily experience, in the created world, and pick up the resonance of God's eternal energy flowing through our beings. *Close to the*

Heart invites you to tune in to this pulse of life, which is constantly flowing through every part of your experience. This is prayer, and it draws the pulse of your daily life into ever-deepening resonance with the heartbeat of God. As you become aware of this resonance, you realize that that secret space at your center is neither empty nor to be feared; it is filled with the love of God, eagerly waiting to flow through every part of your being and into the world in which you live.

PART ONE

Entering Prayer

Prayer invites us to become aware of the living interaction between the transcendent God, who will remain always beyond all we can think or imagine, and the immanent God, who abides deep in our own hearts. As we become aware of this sacred encounter, we become, ourselves, a place where God's dream is becoming incarnate in our own personal human life. We enter into a personal and intimate relationship with the Author of our being.

How can we open ourselves to the possibility of this interaction? How might we approach this call, this desire in our own hearts, for a personal relationship with the One who is closer to us than we are to ourselves and whose dream of us is coming to birth every day of our lives?

This section suggests some ways of entering the heart-depths of prayer.

1

Discovering God inside You

The bean and the blotting paper

✳

Through all the stages of growth, is not the real aim in
life to become ourselves, to allow the barriers to come
down so that the deepest "I" can emerge? . . . To grow
from the seed of life within each of us, rooted in our
earth and history. Is this not our journey home?
— JEAN VANIER, *OUR JOURNEY HOME*

I remember the day, many moons ago, when I was introduced to
the secret of life.

It was all so simple, and it comes back to me today as a model
worth following as we begin this exploration together.

It began with an elementary-school teacher's instruction to
bring a jar and a piece of blotting paper from home to our next
science lesson. In those days jars weren't thrown into the recycling
bin but were washed and stored in the cellar and recycled in the
kitchen every strawberry season. And blotting paper was a house-
hold necessity in the days of pen and ink.

Once our rows of jars were lined up in the classroom, the miracle could begin. The teacher told us to soak our sheets of blotting
paper with tap water and place them as a lining around the inside
of our jars. We were still at the age of wonder, and no one had
spoiled the story for us by telling us the plot in advance. The science teacher came around and gave each of us a bean, which was
clearly going to play some key role in the unfolding drama. We

were then invited to place our beans carefully between the wet blotting paper and the inside surface of our jars.

And that, really, was the end of all demands upon us. We prepared our little trinity of offerings — the jar, the wet blotting paper, and the bean — and the rest was out of our hands.

What happened next was nothing, really. All the teacher did was line up our jars along the windowsill, strategically positioned above the central heating radiators and in the full light of the morning sun. And then we left the experiment to get on with itself.

Everyone knows the rest of the story. A week later when we revisited our jars, each bean had sprouted. Perhaps there is never again quite the thrill of that experiment, when we first observe the beginnings of new life with our own eyes and in our own jars.

The more I think about it, the more it reminds me of prayer.

If we are willing to think small, it isn't too hard to see our day-by-day experience as a piece of blotting paper, soaking up impressions, reactions, events, demands, and responses. And that blotting paper sits (comfortably or otherwise) within our world, the jar.

Then comes the bean — the seed of our uniqueness that will grow into our individual being. This potential is the dream God dreams of us when his love spills over into creation. Our Godseed. Dry and dormant, maybe for many a long year, but one day the moment comes — the "kairos moment" of God's perfect timing, when our experience, soaked through with the living water of the Holy Spirit, sprouts and begins its amazing growth into "Who-I-Am."

And al! we have done is to bring our threefold offering to the place of miracle (which is wherever we happen to find ourselves). We bring our Godseed, our experience, and our world, and we let the Lifemaker do the rest.

We can help the process, both in ourselves and in others. Just as the elementary-school teacher lined up our bean jars along the windowsill above the radiators, so we can bring our raw ingredients to the place of warmth and light.

When it comes to spurring the desire for prayer, a warm place means an accepting, encouraging, and safe space. We place ourselves in a warm space and even generate warmth when we "befriend" the desires of our heart, accepting them just as they are and letting them come to consciousness, welcoming ourselves without judgment or denial or reproach. And we are warmed when we walk alongside others, listening with love and awe as they reveal *their* hearts' deepest desires and inner movements, trusting that we will understand, accept, and affirm them. Heart speaks to heart only where there is such warmth.

And light? If there is any light to be shed, it doesn't come from us. We are like the planets, generating no light of our own, yet able — and called — to *reflect* the light of our Creator. This reflected light is needed if the bean is to come to life. Some of this light comes to us through the prayer-wisdom and practice of the centuries, which has illumined so many pilgrim paths before our own. We can never teach ourselves, or others, to pray, because prayer is a gift, but we *can* receive the light passed on to us from those who have made the journey of prayer ahead of us, and we, in our turn, can pass on something of that light to those who follow after. We can pass it on in the language and the images of our own times and of our own generation's experience of the world.

The light, whether it comes directly from God to the praying heart or is reflected light shared by fellow pilgrims, reaches our Godseed through the glass of the jar. It travels to our hearts through the reality of the created world. The Godseed sprouts and grows right there in our experience, where it has its roots. The various approaches to prayer we will be exploring are firmly grounded in these two places: in our *world* and in our *personal experience*. And they are brought to life by the gifts of warmth and light: gifts that we receive from God and that we also give to each other and to ourselves.

Given these conditions, we, like those seven-year-olds in my science class, will find ourselves once more approaching a miracle. But this time the life we see sprouting is the eternal life that God is calling into fullness in our hearts. Prayer, rooted firmly in *where-we-are*, yet striving for *where-we-long-to-be*, is the expression of that heart-call — God's call to us — and our response.

We can see the miracle with our own eyes. We can watch it happening in our own jars. And once we have seen its beginnings in our hearts and have started to notice its effects in the way we live and relate to one another, we will know that we have tapped into the secret of Life.

I hope, through this book, to offer a little warmth and a little light. The jar is all around us, in the created world in which we live and the political world in which we operate, with all its glory and its shame. You will need to bring along the blotting paper of your daily experience, soaked as it already is with the living water of God's Spirit that has been springing within you since your life began. You bring also your Godseed, of course — the bean that is uniquely and irreplaceably *you* among all the other fifty-seven times fifty-seven varieties. This Godseed is already sprouting and striving for all that it is becoming, in God.

Equipped with these raw materials, we might explore together some ways of adventuring into personal prayer, enjoying the warmth of good companionship as we make this pilgrimage of the heart, and letting a little light shine in still undiscovered places.

❊ TAKING IT FURTHER ❊

Life is a bakery

I once heard that "truth is delivered to us daily, fresh-baked in the ovens of our own experience." Try dwelling on the picture these words evoke for you. Try making friends with your "oven" — your everyday experience. Reflect on the possibility that the walls that seem to enclose you, the heat and frenzy that seem to stifle you, and the delays and frustrations that seem to hold you back may be the very means of revealing the truth that is already in your life.

Sit still

Allow yourself to be still for five or ten minutes, alone if possible, in a place where you feel comfortable. Relax and simply enjoy this time of being *you*, free for a while of the many demands on you by other people to fit into their plans and structures. Let yourself be like the bean, whose only purpose is to grow into what it really is.

The internal blueprint

Reflect on the innermost kernel that contains your unique, eternal blueprint. Can you recognize what or who is providing, or has ever provided, warmth and light for you? Perhaps you recall particular times and places that have made you feel especially alive. Or you remember particular people who have (perhaps quite unconsciously) spoken a word or sparked an idea or response in you that you now see was life-giving, or even life-changing.

Let your memories float free. Enjoy them. Draw on the energy they have released in you. Allow them to be food for your journey.

2

Listening to God

Receiving or transmitting?

※

*When you listen with your soul, you come into rhythm
and unity with the music of the universe.*
— JOHN O'DONOHUE, *ANAM CARA* —
SPIRITUAL WISDOM FROM THE CELTIC WORLD

On my way to work, I pass a radio telescope. Every time I pass, it seems to be in a different position: sometimes flat, with its huge dish raised to the skies like a soup bowl, and sometimes almost upright, as if searching out some stray star that is just about to slip beyond the horizon. Sometimes I see it laboriously moving, its huge bulk creaking heavily up or down, left or right.

Whenever I pass this telescope, it reminds me of prayer. Prayer can be pretty heavy-going too. Or so it seems, especially if we go at it in the ways so many of us were taught as children. Depending on your Christian tradition, you may have learned that, to be effective, prayer must be painful. Stiff limbs and aching knees were part of the package, and the rest was often a test of memory. Perhaps the worst of it was the awful sense of guilt that overcame you when you forgot (or willfully omitted) your prayers or found, at the end of prayer time, that you had been away in some fantasy and couldn't rightly remember what you had said.

Perhaps I am projecting my shortcomings onto you. Maybe your early experience of prayer was entirely satisfactory. A child who learns to pray in a parent's embrace, for example, has a head start when it comes to relating to a loving God.

No matter how you learned to pray, you will have your own reasons for picking up this book and looking, perhaps, for some new approach to your personal life of prayer. Whatever those reasons are, I would like to invite you back to the radio telescope. It reminds me of the huge, complicated efforts we make to catch the signals of the stars. But it also reminds me that all we can do to receive God is direct our hearts towards God and trust him to do the rest.

That satellite dish spells out for me a few simple ground rules:

• Prayer is *God's initiative,* not our achievement.

• Prayer is about *listening* more than about talking.

• Prayer is about *receiving* more than about making requests.

• Prayer is about *coming to rest while pointed in God's direction.*

The satellite dish can do nothing more than direct itself toward the source of the signal. It can't force the signal to happen. All its efforts are directed toward receiving the signal and interpreting it in ways that mean something for life on Earth. Prayer is like that. We can open ourselves up to it and remain alert to it. We can receive it and reflect on what it means for our daily living. We can act on it and let it inform our choices and decisions. But we cannot force it, because prayer is *God's gift,* and, however carefully we prepare for it, it will always take us by surprise, which, after all, is what real gifts are supposed to do!

And how might we set about opening ourselves up to receive God in this sort of way? I would suggest that we do this in exactly the same way as we would open our hearts to a dear friend. *We listen.* And we ask for the grace to listen with our full attention and with the trust and expectation that we would have in a conversation with our friend. To listen like this requires a degree of stillness and silence that doesn't always come naturally in our world of feverish and anxious activity and busyness.

Ten Feet Down

A friend once told me an interesting fact. During a storm at sea, the water ten feet below the trough of the highest wave is perfectly calm. The picture appealed to me, and it helps me come to prayer.

Like most people, I live most of my life on the surface of myself. My conscious journey through a typical day is mainly occupied with the "waves." Sometimes they are manageable. Sometimes they reach storm force, and at the end of the day I feel exhausted and fraught. Yet this stillness, if my friend is right, lies just "ten feet down." That doesn't seem like an impossible depth to reach. Might we use this image for ourselves when we are seeking the stillness of heart in which prayer can happen?

Through the ages, men and women have sought this close communion with God that we call prayer, and almost all traditions of faith and spiritual searching have realized that prayer depends on *stillness*. The purpose of stilling ourselves is to bring us down to the deeper currents of our hearts. Here we can notice what we are really feeling, what is moving us at this level of our being, and where these feelings and movements come from. And it is precisely in those deep currents that God is speaking to our hearts, revealing our innermost desires and fears to us, inviting us to reach toward our truest desires and to surrender our fears and hurts to God's healing.

Surrender! A challenging word and an act of faith in itself. Because when we still ourselves and sink ten feet down, we are acknowledging that we are not our own managers. We are acknowledging that our surface thoughts and preoccupations — and even our images of God and notions of how prayer ought to be — can be obstacles to our meeting with God in the furthest reaches of ourselves. Prayer is an act of surrender. It asks us to let go of our own agenda and listen to God.

When we surrender, we take a risk. We make ourselves open to God's suggestions. We do so in an act of faith, trusting that God will pour himself into our stillness and fill us with his Spirit. When this happens, we can no more predict the consequences than the astronomer can specify in advance what the skies will reveal through the telescope and what implications those revelations may have for life on Earth. This is the cost, and the adventure, of the inner journey.

Tuning In

Once it is in the right position, the telescope becomes passive; it simply waits there, open and receptive. There is really only one active moment in this whole procedure: The telescope needs to be *focused* on the place where the signal is expected to be found. This question of focusing lies, I believe, at the heart of prayer. When you are engaged in an intimate conversation with a friend, you will probably not be gazing out of the window or concentrating on the state of your fingernails or reading the newspaper. You will more likely be looking at your friend eye to eye. And you won't even be aware that you are focusing so deeply on your friend, because your attention is no longer on *yourself* and on how well you are doing in the interchange, but on your friend and what he or she is revealing to you.

This is often a fundamental difference between the ways we have learned to pray and the kind of prayer that is truly directed toward God. There is prayer that centers around my words, my petitions, what I want God to do for me. And there is prayer that sinks into stillness and surrenders to God. This book suggests some ways of coming to this deep stillness and explores some ways of focusing our hearts on God. And we may discover that we are no longer "saying our prayers" but, rather, *listening to* them.

As we sink into this focused stillness, the teeming questions that normally fill our minds are gradually relinquished as our own efforts lessen and our receptivity sharpens. No longer: "Where am I? What is happening to me? How must I do things?"

But simply: "Be still, and know that I am God" (Psalm 46:10 KJV).

❦ TAKING IT FURTHER ❦

Find a sacred space

At this early stage in our explorations, the most important thing is the discovery of our own inner stillness. This is the quiet place in our hearts where God can speak to us and where we can listen and hear.

Try remembering a place and a time where you have been deeply happy and at peace. Let the scene come back to you. Remember where it was, what the weather was like, what season of the year it was. Were you alone or with someone else? Feel the sun, or the rain, again on your cheeks. Smell the scents of the place. Hear its sounds. Go back there in your imagination, quite deliberately, and be quiet with your memories for a few minutes. In your own way, express your gratitude to God for this remembered experience. Invite God to come to you again in that memory and to make that place a *sacred space* for you. A sacred space is quite simply a space where you can become more fully aware of God's presence.

These few minutes that you have spent with your memory *are* prayer. Be still, in the recognition that you have met God in your sacred space. Your telescope has come to rest in a place where it feels focused on God. Perhaps you have come into this exercise thinking, *I can't pray.* Now savor the joy of discovering that you *can* pray, and that it didn't hurt at all!

Now that you have discovered a sacred space in your memory and in your heart, return to it as often as you feel drawn to do so. This could be in a time of reflection on the bus going to work, in the grocery checkout line, or over the kitchen sink. Go back to your space, but as you do so, ask God to meet you there. He is the One who first gave you the experience you have just remembered. Show God your joy in receiving it. Your own joy is only a fraction of *his* joy in receiving your response. If you doubt this, remember how you have felt when you have given a child a gift and the child responded happily. In such a situation, whose joy is greater — yours or the child's?

If you practice this stilling exercise whenever you can, in all of
the frenzy, you are sure to notice little pockets of calm. Your days
will have been touched by prayer. Depending on your circumstances, you might like to find a corner of your home or maybe
another spot where you feel at ease and where you can be alone.
If you can, make this little corner into a prayer space. The space
might have more significance to you if you place a candle there or
a cross, picture, or flowers and your Bible. This will become your
focal point for a set-aside time of prayer.

Don't worry if this doesn't seem to be possible. Not all families
offer individual family members the luxury of this kind of privacy!
If this isn't for you, there are many other ways of marking a place
in your life as prayer space. Try putting some small reminder of
your desire for God in the car or on your desk or in the kitchen
with the detergents or on the bathroom shelf. It doesn't have to
be anything religious. It may be much more powerful as a symbol
if it is something ordinary that expresses your personal relationship with God.

For my birthday one year, my daughter gave me a little string
hammock cradling a furry toy. I have it hanging on the window
by my desk. Other people may see it as a toy, but for me it is a reminder that I am held in God's unfailing love. When things get
frantic, it nudges me to see myself in that cradling hammock of
God's love. Little things like this are ways of returning to prayer
over and over again, right in the middle of "real life."

Satellite dish

This second exercise is intended to help you turn the dish of your
inner telescope toward God (and, therefore, away from yourself).
This may sound easy, but actually it is very difficult to wrench
the focus away from self and toward the other, whether the other
is God or a human person. It is hard because it means facing our
human tendency to relate to others in terms of how they are affecting us. Some people make us feel good. Some disturb us, annoy
us, or antagonize us. Some seem well-meaning, and others seem

to want to undermine us. If we look at these sorts of feelings toward others, we have to admit that they are about "how *we* feel."

Empathy lies at the heart of all true listening. Empathy is, I believe, about making that radical switch of focus from "I" to the "other." If we can really feel as the other feels, if, as the old saying goes, we can "walk a mile in his shoes," then we are *beginning* to learn to focus our hearts and to love with God's love. So the exercise is this:

Try noticing one or two of the conversations or personal encounters you have each day. It doesn't matter whether the other people are friendly or not-so-friendly. Just become aware of them. Begin by reflecting on one or two encounters each day before you go to sleep. (With practice you may be able to develop this awareness at the time of the conversation.) Ask yourself: *Where was my focus, for the most part, during this conversation?* On myself or on the other person? A word of warning: Don't be discouraged if you find over and over again that the focus is mainly on yourself. Welcome to the human race! Almost no one practices real empathy in their dealings with others. But we can learn to do so, and our finest teacher is Jesus.

Try reflecting on one or two Gospel incidents. Let Jesus show you how *he* relates to others; notice especially where his focus is in these conversations:

- Matthew 14:22 – 33. Jesus walks on the water. Notice what happens to Peter's focus here.

- Matthew 19:13 – 15. Jesus is with the little children. Where is Jesus' focus? Where is the focus of the disciples?

- Luke 18:35 – 43. Where is the blind man's focus? How does Jesus change this? Reflect especially on verse 41: "What do you want me to do for you?"

Do you have a relationship in which you feel empathy (at least from time to time)? In the better moments of family life, for example, a person may genuinely feel the pain or the joy of a child or of an elderly relative; in doing so, the empathic person is able to go beyond his or her own interests. John the Baptist realized this need for complete refocusing when he said, in John 3:30: "He must grow greater, I must grow less."

Find and treasure any moments of empathy in your daily experience — your empathy with another or another person's empathy with you — and *ask God to imprint on your heart how it feels when you are relating to another person in this way.* You may discover gifts in the day, such as the phone call from someone who cares enough to ask how you really are or that lurch of pain inside you when you hear a child being unjustly harangued by an overwrought parent. Such moments lead us to empathy, to genuine "holy listening." These moments point us to the heart of God.

3

Sinking into Silence

Ways to inner stillness

✳

Prayer is the means by which I open myself up to that which is not me.

— ALAN JONES, SOUL MAKING

Ten feet down — that magic depth that my friend suggested to me as the place where the water is still — might as well be on another planet for most of us, most of the time. Our lives are tossed about relentlessly by the turbulence of the surface waves. How do we learn to sink down those ten crucial feet into the stillness at the center of ourselves? How might we encourage that deep inner relaxation that is the sign of surrender and openness to whatever God may wish to show us?

This chapter looks at a few approaches to help us practice becoming inwardly still. For many people, this time of stillness becomes a natural part of their day, a space for restoring perspective in an overcrowded life. With practice, the habit can grow into the ability to find stillness at any time, in the many little spaces that our lives reveal.

Preparing for Prayer

Before you engage in a time of relaxed prayerfulness, it is good to stop for a moment and remember what you are about to do. You are approaching God, the Lord of all creation, and asking him

17

for the gift of prayer, through his Holy Spirit. You might find it helpful to mark this moment of humble petition in some personal way. For example, I have a little pot of scented ointment. Each day at my prayer time, I "anoint" my forehead to remind myself that I am asking to come, in prayer, into the presence of God. This in itself helps to steady me into stillness and reflectiveness. Another helpful way of marking the start of prayer is by lighting a candle and spending a few moments in its light.

There are many ways of relaxing; you no doubt have your favorite method. There is no need to practice complicated techniques or to take any expensive courses! Relaxing is just what it says it is. Find a comfortable place, perhaps a reasonably firm chair. Sit upright, but not rigidly, so that your back is straight and your feet are placed firmly on the floor. Rest your hands loosely in your lap or on your knees, whatever feels right for you. You may like to close your eyes. Or, if this feels more natural for you, focus your gaze on some object that will attract your wandering thoughts without distracting you — maybe a candle, flower, picture, icon, or cross that has personal meaning for you. For example, I have an open oyster shell and a special stone that I sometimes use to help me focus.

Entering Sacred Space

In chapter 2 we looked at a way of discovering a sacred space in your imagination by using your memory. Many people find this kind of memory a useful gateway into meditative prayer. I have one friend, for example, who often goes, in prayer, to a particular path in her imagination that leads to a park bench. She sits down there and meets Jesus in her own way. She often tells me what her morning trip to the bench revealed to her! Other people go to an imaginary room inside themselves and close the door (as Jesus himself told us to do when we pray); there they are alone in their meeting with the Lord.

Another friend, who lives in a city with a boisterous family, has no space to call her own except the view from the window of her second-floor apartment. But from that window she can see a particular tree, which accompanies her prayer all through the year, from the cloudy white of blossom time, through all the greens of spring and summer and the yellows and browns of autumn, to the stark, bare winter branches. The tree is often her soul friend when she has no other. The Celts held certain significant places to be especially sacred. These included wells, springs, boundaries of all kinds, bridges, doorways, and causeways.

When you reflect on your own life's geography, do you notice any places that have this kind of significance for you? Your "places" may be specific memories or experiences; sacred space is often discovered in our own experience and our own story. Consider:

- times when you have felt that you were at the bottom of the well but where, in fact, you have discovered living water that has given you a fresh start in life;

- times when you have felt new energy springing up in you;

- times when you have felt you were walking at the extremities of experience, perhaps times of great suffering or intense joy;

- times when you have felt you were in transition between two phases of your life, as if crossing a bridge or a causeway toward an unknown future;

- times when you have felt you were standing in front of a closed door, which later turned out to be a gateway to a time of growth.

The memory of any of these may help you enter the sacred space within yourself. Simply let the memory arise, unhampered, and ask God to consecrate it for you. Let it become the starting point for your prayer and your descent ten feet down.

Some people find it helpful to take off their shoes on entering what they sense to be the sacred space in which they meet God in a special way.

Your Body—Your Ally

In all this talk of imagination and memory, we are in danger of forgetting that we are all embodied creatures and that our physical beings are as much a part of our prayer as our thoughts, feelings, and memories.

One sacred space is always there for you, wherever and however you live, and that is your own body. With just a little, gentle training, your body can be your friend, ally, and faithful collaborator in the great adventure of prayer. The body that feels so full of itches and aches, the brain that is only waiting for a chance to rush off to attend to the day's agenda, and the senses that want to wander off after every sound and smell can actually *help* you enter prayer. Here are a few ways in which this can happen. You might like to try them out and use any one that appeals to you on a particular day:

- Try tensing all your muscles and then letting them go, one by one, becoming conscious of how each part of you is becoming relaxed and "letting go."

- Concentrate on one part of your body—let's say, your little toe. Either stay with that one part for as long as you can or gradually move your attention to each part of your body in turn. Become aware of how each part is feeling and of any discomfort or other sensation, such as the pressure of your shoe or the chair against your back.

- Notice your own breathing. Become fully conscious of every breath, as you breathe in and as you breathe out. When you breathe out, let all your surface worries and preoccupations go, one by one. (Think of them as you let them go, and deliberately surrender them out of your control and into God's.) When you breathe in, take into yourself the peace of God. Let the steady rhythm of your breathing calm you and bring you into a natural balance.

- Become aware of your own pulse or heartbeat. As you notice each beat of your heart, reflect that God is holding you through every second of your life, for "in him we live, and move, and have our being" (Acts 17:28 KJV).

• Use a mantra, or a simple word or phrase that speaks to you in some way, to steady your mind into silence. Choose a phrase like *Maranatha* or its English equivalent *Come, Lord Jesus* and repeat it over and over until it becomes almost like breathing. This is a way of occupying the upper levels of your mind and leaving the deeper reaches of yourself free to be present to the silence of prayer.

• Listen very attentively to the sounds around you. Begin with the noises in the outside world — the traffic, the birds, the neighbors. Then move your attention to your own room. Listen to the humming of the radiator, the gurgling of the pipes, the creaking of the wood. Finally, bring your attention into your own body and become aware of the sounds within you, especially your heartbeat.

Inner stillness can, paradoxically, often be found in action. Swimming is an excellent opportunity for prayer. If you enjoy swimming, you may find that your half hour in the pool can become an oasis of prayer in itself. Let the water support you; become aware of its buoyancy beneath you, just as God's love supports you. Notice the center of gravity in yourself as you move steadily through the water; realize that the whole exercise is one of balance. Far more important than the sometimes wild movements of your arms and legs is this deep center of gravity, which holds you in harmony and in balance with the water. Of course you don't think about it when you are swimming, and neither are you conscious of this balance when you pray, but this invisible pivot point is nevertheless the inner compass that governs your movement. The action of swimming can also act as a physical mantra, keeping your mental processes occupied with the one operation of swimming and leaving the rest of you free to follow the call of prayer.

Steady walking can have the same effect and is another way of expressing an inner desire to be directed toward God and beyond yourself. You may find it helpful to use a verbal mantra along with your walking. For example, you could match the rhythm of your steps to a phrase such as the scriptural "in you I live, and move, and have my being."

And after Prayer

It is helpful to close your prayer period with a familiar prayer, such as The Lord's Prayer, which also acts as a reminder that, although we pray individually, we are also praying, constantly, in community. As one hymn says, "the voice of prayer is never silent" as Earth spins. All who seek God are part of an unceasing circle of prayer. As one person ends his prayer, another is just beginning. Using a prayer shared by all as a conclusion to your personal prayer reminds you of your place in the entire communion of faith.

Those who are familiar with Roman Catholic practices may find helpful the gesture of making a small sign of the cross on the forehead, the lips, and the heart. This is commonly done by individuals just before the Gospel is read during the Mass. Not being a "cradle Catholic" myself, I have never established exactly what it is supposed to signify, but I have long since discovered my own meanings for it. I use this gesture frequently at the end of a period of prayer, and at the start of a new day, to express my desire for God's blessing today on "every thought in my head, every word on my lips, and every stirring in my heart." I add a fourth "sign of the cross" to the back of my hand, to express the desire for a blessing on "everything I write and every task I do today."

But I feel it is important not to let such habits or gestures become automatic or mechanical, which could cause them to degenerate into superstitious practices. Let them come from your heart, if they come at all. Let them express what you really desire.

If you have been using a candle, when you blow it out watch and smell the smoke as it rises and disappears into the air. Your prayer will do that too. It will seem to have finished and disappeared. But in reality it will have become part of the very air you breathe. It will have slipped silently, but fragrantly, into your life and into the life of all creation. It will have become a carrier of grace for the whole human family. You will go forward into your daily life carrying its power in your heart in very real, though invisible, ways, which I hope will become clearer to you as we move forward in this venture.

❧ TAKING IT FURTHER ❧

Mud in a glass

Imagine your desire for stillness, both inner and outer, as a glass of muddy water. You might see this glass as the container of your consciousness. In its shaken, disturbed state, it is opaque, useless, and potentially harmful. But as you sink into prayer (and the mud in the glass settles), watch the cloudiness sink with you.

Ever so gradually the water at the top of the glass becomes clear again, and the mud sinks deeper.

Notice how the band of clear water widens and the layer of mud narrows at the bottom of the glass, even as it settles and thickens in density.

Eventually the stilling, settling process is complete. The water in the glass is pure, giving you clarity of vision and wholesome water to quench your inner thirst (and perhaps to give to others who are thirsty).

And the mud? A place, perhaps, where God will plant the seed of something new. Both elements are part of God's plan: our clarity and purity, and our mud. Only our own confusion clouds the issue.

Combing the beach

Coming to stillness in prayer can feel a bit like beach combing, walking slowly along the shoreline, noticing the movement of the waves and the brush of the breeze on your skin, all the while alert to whatever treasure may have been left at your feet by the tide.

Imagine the shoreline of your life, stretching out behind you and ahead of you. Notice the waves breaking constantly over the shore, like the waves of your day-by-day experience, in restless motion, occupying almost all of your consciousness almost all of the time.

How are the waves today? Perhaps they are gentle, asking only for a little space to land and break. Or perhaps they are heaving like gray mountains, swelling and straining with pain and the unmanageable forces of their own energy. Maybe they are sparkling in the sunlight today, scattering happiness like foam across the rocks, or maybe they are creeping in tears, seeking comfort in God's presence, begging for shelter until the tide turns.

However they are, simply let them be there. Become attentive to that sacred space where the waves of your life meet the steady shore of God's presence. Know that you are welcome there, seeking God on your shoreline. Feel free to wander like a beachcomber, just for the joy of it. From time to time, however, there will be gifts on the sand, waiting to be discovered and gratefully gathered. As you wander, receive God's personal blessings upon your life as though they were special shells. A word in Scripture, perhaps, that speaks to your heart, or a memory that arises, or a moment of calm where there was turbulence.

The tide will ebb again, and your meeting with the Lord may seem to have been sucked out to sea, but it will not leave you unchanged. You will no longer be who you were a prayer ago nor yet who you will be another prayer away, beyond the next tide's turning. There may be a long day ahead, until the tide of prayer can flow again, but the rock of God's presence remains immovable. Only the tides of life move in and out.

ADDITIONAL READING

Sadhana — A Way to God, by Anthony de Mello, S.J. (New York: Doubleday, Image, 1984).

4

Making Connections

The bridge between prayer and daily life

✳

When I did manage to keep awake and make some
kind of prayer, I often felt the activity was like riding a
bicycle without a chain, for what I was doing in prayer
seemed to have little connection with everyday life.
— GERARD HUGHES, *OH GOD, WHY?*

My time of prayer this morning was very peaceful, very healing,
but I can't actually remember a thing about it."

Does this kind of comment ring any bells with you? "My time
of prayer" might also read "my day of recollection" or even "my
retreat." The problem is familiar to many of us. Prayer seems,
sometimes, to "go in one ear and out the other." We know that it
was a good thing, but we don't begin to understand why it was
good or what effect it may have had on us. Over the years I have
heard so many people lament the fact that the time they have
given to meditation and stillness has seemed to flow on, like a
river, leaving behind no apparent trace of itself in their lives. This
experience can, sadly, seduce us into giving up on prayer or letting it lapse into mere daydreaming.

We are seriously missing the point when we look for "results"
from our prayer. As long as we are expecting some kind of pay-
back, the focus will remain firmly on ourselves and our hopes and
expectations — and not on God. We will be concentrating, as
Teresa of Avila put it, on "the consolations of God" rather than

25

on "the God of consolations." Nevertheless, prayer, if it is authentic, *will* make a difference to us — to our way of making decisions and of being human in the surroundings in which we find ourselves. But that difference may become apparent to us only over time and as a result of patient observation, as we notice God's action in our lives and the ways in which he may be encouraging, warning, and challenging us. We will notice these things not so much during prayer itself, when our focus will be on God for God's own sake, but in the time *after* prayer when we stop to reflect on what seems to have been happening during the prayer.

There are two practices that can help change a ritual of saying our prayers or meditating into an authentic and life-giving encounter with our deepest selves in God.

- After prayer we can consciously reflect (in our minds) on what has been happening during prayer (in our hearts).

- We can make conscious connections between our prayer and our experience and between the story of God's self-expression, particularly in Scripture, and the mystery of God's self-expression in our own lives and personalities.

Cut and Dried?

A farmer friend told me one day that according to an old tradition, the cut corn at harvest time was supposed to lie in the fields to dry until the church bells had rung across it three times, that is, three Sundays.

As my friend gave me this piece of wisdom, the phrase *cut and dried* came to my mind. It made me wonder about my own ways of discerning things and making decisions. I saw that my decisions and so-called discernments usually get cut and gathered on the same day, with no time for maturing — so sure am I of my own judgments!

But the habit of reflection can make a difference. It can slow us down just long enough to make a short space of time after prayer "for the corn to dry" before we rush off to meet the demands of the day. It provides an opportunity to let our own feelings about our prayer time come to the surface — a chance to stand back and notice how the time has been, gathering any fruits of that time that come to mind. It may be all we need to ensure that our prayer is not only cut but dried as well, so that it has time and space to mature and become more fully a part of our lives.

The Practice of Reflection

Time for reflection really needn't be a burden. If you can find the extra five or ten minutes, bring your prayer time to a close and then make a deliberate break, perhaps by moving to a different place or making yourself a cup of coffee. Then settle for just a few minutes and notice:

How did you go into the time of prayer? What issues were in your mind? How were you feeling? Tired, fresh, energetic, or unwell? How long did you intend to give to prayer? How did you focus your prayer? Did you use a passage of Scripture, for example? What particular "grace" or gift, or guidance were you asking for or desiring? What were you hoping for from your time of prayer?

What were your feelings during the time of prayer? How was the time for you — comfortable or uncomfortable, short or long, tedious or interesting, turbulent or peaceful? Did you notice any movements of mood or feeling during the prayer time? Did anything in the prayer trigger feelings of elation, despondency, hope, or anxiety? Were you able to express these feelings to God and to yourself?

How do you feel now, looking back over the time of prayer?

- Did you spend the time in prayer that you originally intended to spend? Many praying people sense that it isn't so important to pray for a particular length of time, but rather to stay *faithful to* whatever time you have decided to set aside. Try to resist the temptation to cut short the period you have decided upon. Prayer often comes alive at the very end of the time you have given to it.

- Do you feel you have received the grace you were asking for? (Keep an open mind about this last question; sometimes the grace you asked for comes in ways and at times you least expect it, often as you go on with your day, but it is good to remind yourself, in reflection, what you were actually seeking in your prayer.)

- Is there anything in the time of prayer that "draws you back"? Anything you feel you would like to return to next time? Any unfinished business?

- Is there anything in your prayer that you especially want to store in your memory? Did anything (in Scripture, for example) connect to where you feel you are in your present experience?

If your daily schedule simply doesn't allow for this ideal situation of ten minutes' quiet reflection over a cup of coffee, this needn't become a problem. *Everything we are exploring in this heart pilgrimage is going to be discovered in our daily lives, just as they are, just as we are living them.* The kitchen, the computer workstation, the coffee shop—these are our cloisters, and this is where we will find the God of all things. Your reflection can be woven into your day and picked up again and again, whenever you have a free minute. Just let the awareness of your time with God float at the edges of your consciousness, so that it can surface whenever there is a relevant prompt. You may find, for example, that things happen, or are said, during the day that bring to life something that arose in your prayer. These things may go a long way toward deepening your prayer experience, giving it real meaning in your life and helping you notice how the grace you are desiring is being given, gift wrapped in God's surprises.

You might find it helpful to make a short note of anything striking that arises from your reflection. This is particularly important if you are sharing your journey with a soul friend (see chapter 23). Keeping a notebook of your reflections can help you focus in later conversations with a companion. It can also help you see how your encounter with God has been moving through the weeks and months and years, how issues have been resolved over time, how you have grown in faith and hope and love. In this way the corn continues to ripen as it lies in the field waiting for the threefold chimes of the church bells.

Connecting and Reconnecting: Crossing the Causeway

One of the most wonderful graces of reflection is that it gives us the space in which to notice how prayer is connecting with our present reality.

To explore this process of connection, let's "go to" a place that was in many ways a cradle of prayer in the islands of Britain. If you were to follow in the steps of Saint Aidan and Saint Cuthbert (both of them saintly, unassuming, seventh-century Celtic monks who brought the gospel from Scotland to the north of England), you would find yourself on a small tidal island in the North Sea, just off the coast of Northumberland. To get to this island, the Holy Island of Lindisfarne, you would have to wait for low tide to cross the sands of the causeway, which is accessible for only a few hours between the tides.

A causeway is revered as an especially sacred place in the Celtic mind and heart. It is a place of transition, a means of passing from where you are to where you desire to be. In this sense, you might with truth call a causeway a channel of grace. But it is also a powerful parable of prayer. In your imagination let the tide ebb and then walk quietly across the causeway, as if you were walking into the sacred space of silence and prayer. Is there anything specific, any issue in your life, that you are carrying with you today from the mainland to the island? If so, simply let it be there with you, without making any deliberate effort to "resolve" it. Allow the stillness of the holy place to receive you, welcome you, enfold you. And as you sink into the stillness, allow the tide to come in and encircle you in your island-space. Slowly the causeway disappears, submerged by the rising tides. You are alone with God on the island of your prayer.

Eventually the tide turns. Your time of prayer is over. The water recedes. The causeway reappears. It is time for the return journey, back to the mainland. Perhaps you are eager to return, relieved that the time of prayer has passed, if it has been difficult or dry. Perhaps you are reluctant to return, wishing that the island-time could last forever. Either way, the mainland beckons you. It is time to *reconnect* to the place of your daily life.

What do you carry with you as you return to the mainland? Will your memory of the island-time be washed away with the incoming tide, like footprints on the sands? Or is there something you would like to gather and keep as food for the onward journey? What happened on the island that will change the way you make choices and relationships on the mainland?

Living the Fifth Gospel

The picture of the island, connected to the mainland by its causeway, can help open up a different kind of "way" in our hearts, submerged as they are for so much of the time beneath life's flood. Prayer, and the reflection that follows it, can reveal our personal gospel story — each pilgrim's "fifth gospel." Prayer and reflection can lead us into an intimate friendship with the Lord and suggest ways of living out that friendship in God's world.

I have a friend, for example, whose life could be called a minefield. She has experienced far more than her share of hardship and heartbreak, yet the light of her spirit seems to shine out of her, unhindered. One morning, after I had seen this friend, the daily lectionary reading was the story of Jesus sending his disciples off in a boat across the sea. A horrible storm came up, and Jesus came walking across the water to them just as they thought they were about to go under. As I let this Gospel story form my prayer, my friend came to mind. The picture that presented itself in my imagination was of a lighthouse, steadily beaming out its promise of courage and hope while surrounded by tempestuous seas. My friend was such a lighthouse.

But it was afterwards, as I reflected on the prayer, that the connections came to life. Did I want to be a lighthouse? Could I be a lighthouse? Lighthouses — aren't they constructed on the most dangerous rocks or sand banks? My thoughts turned to my own life and a particular reluctance to risk a specific rocky hazard. I was led to reflect on the cost — in terms of risk and of loneliness — of being a lighthouse. I was challenged to ask myself whether I was prepared to pay such a price in my own circumstances. Did I want to be a lighthouse? (A lighthouse planted safely inland in a sheltered grove is no use at all!)

In this example, the process of *reflection* helped me notice the ways in which God was moving through my feelings and my memories during this particular time of prayer. Reflection helped me recognize the places in which he was stirring up my attention and challenging my response. And the process of *connection* gave me some solid guidelines on how to take this truth into my experience and make it incarnate. It was helping me learn, perhaps, a new way of dealing with an old difficulty.

⚓ TAKING IT FURTHER ⚓

One important thing

When your attention is focused on something specific, you may well become aware of that "something" far more often than you normally would. For example, if you are waiting for a ride with someone who drives a red car, you will be amazed at how many red cars there are on the roads! We have a large spruce tree in our front garden, and I often used to tell people about it as a landmark to look for if they were trying to find our home for the first time — until one disgruntled visitor told me just how many spruce trees he had counted in other people's front gardens before locating ours!

We can make use of this tendency when reflecting on our prayer. Try remembering just one important thing about your prayer and carrying it through the day with you. Possibly you were feeling unexpectedly elated, or dejected, by something that arose in prayer. Or maybe you noticed a particular connection between something in Scripture and something in your own life. Just carry it with you, whatever it is, and notice any moments during the day when the same kind of thing comes into your awareness. Each time this happens, allow it to deepen your prayer, as an artist might add touches of color and shading, bit by bit, to a picture she has begun.

Backwards and forwards

Make friends with your "causeway." Gradually let yourself become familiar with the feeling of moving backwards and forwards between the island (your prayer) and the mainland (your daily life). Notice the rhythm of your own tides and the natural interactions between high tide, when you are alone with God on the island, and low tide, when you are wholly engaged with the demands and strains of your personal circumstances. Notice, and perhaps make a written note of, any issues you are carrying from the mainland to the island, and any gifts you are taking back from the island to the mainland. Are these gifts for yourself, do you think, or for other people as well?

Welcome this trade route in your heart and let it become fruitful. Become more aware of what you are hoping for from it and how these hopes are being fulfilled.

5

Focusing on True Desires

"What are you looking for?"

※

Our most authentic desires spring ultimately from the deep wells of our being where the longing for God runs freely.
— PHILIP SHELDRAKE, *BEFRIENDING OUR DESIRES*

John 1:35 – 39 tells of two men, former disciples of John the Baptist and just introduced to Jesus. They turn to follow Jesus and are stopped in their tracks when he turns around to face them, looks straight into their eyes, and asks them this question: "What are you looking for?"

If you can imagine yourself in their position, how do *you* feel when the Lord holds your gaze and asks you what you are really looking for by following him? His eyes seem to search out your innermost desires. Dare you do the same?

The disciples are thrown by the question. Perhaps they cast around in their minds for some appropriate answer. What comes out is just another question: "Where do you live, Rabbi?" To which he invites them into a life-changing journey: "Come and see!"

Like the disciples, each of us has in some way made the first tentative steps to follow the One who beckons. We know a little of where we are coming from, but nothing of where we are going. Perhaps we hesitate, reluctant to take the next step into the beyond without some assurance that our Leader at least has a map. He offers us no such assurance. Quite the reverse. He turns instead and places the unanswered question back in our own hearts: *What are you looking for?*

Asking for What You Desire

We are not the first pilgrims to be disconcerted by this question. Through the centuries many believers have discovered how difficult it can be to notice what one is really seeking and simply to ask God for it. In some traditions this is called "asking for the grace." All it means is noticing where your own desire — in this particular prayer — is *focused* and naming that desire to God in your prayer.

It all sounds very simple, in theory. In practice it can look quite different. I remember the first time I was faced with the question myself. I was making my first retreat. On the first morning my retreat guide asked me exactly that: "What grace are you seeking in your prayer today?" I was as floored as those first disciples must have been! It had never occurred to me to ask God for what I wanted, and I realized that I didn't have any clear idea myself about what I wanted or hoped to gain from the day's prayer. And, frankly, at the time I couldn't see why it should be so important. Surely I could safely leave it all with God, who, after all, knew far better than I did what I wanted and what I needed.

Of course the exercise is not at all about informing God of our needs and desires. Rather, and much more necessarily, it is about bringing these needs and desires up from our own unconscious depths into the realms of consciousness so that *we* become aware of them. When we "ask for what we desire" we are actually pinpointing the real kernel of our own desiring.

Why do our own desires matter so much? And why are we sometimes so reluctant to express them?

Divine Discontent

When asked, "What do you desire?" people's reactions vary enormously. Some will deny that they have any desires at all, because they believe that as Christians they should be content with whatever life gives them. Others find that there are so many desires milling around in their hearts that they don't know where to begin.

And almost all of us have an uneasy feeling about our desires, having grown up feeling that we should be suppressing our own desires in an attempt to seek "God's Will." Many of us have been strongly influenced by the idea that a personal desire is somehow a bad thing or, at the very least, untrustworthy and likely to seduce us into error. God's Will (whatever that is), on the other hand, can be trusted—if only it were not so unhelpfully invisible!

The very word *desire* carries connotations of sin, while the word *will* seems to carry weight and authority, however oppressive. The programming goes deep into our hearts and minds that if we are enjoying something it must be wrong and that an iron will, reflected in an iron face, is more likely to be morally acceptable.

Yet we believe that God *desires* us into being. He *desires* our wholeness so much that he allows himself to be broken for its sake. He awakens our desire for him by pouring his own Spirit into our lives. Our hearts *long for* him, we say, just as a river seeks its ocean home. The whole of creation lives and grows under the impulse of desire. Every new life springs from a moment of desire. Every flower is pollinated by attraction and desire. Every step of discovery is made out of a desire to go beyond, always beyond, the horizon of the known. Every meal we eat, the very sustenance of our living, is taken because our bodies express their need of food in the desire that we call appetite.

Why, then, do we feel the need to suppress our own desires? Is it possible that our deepest desires flow in the same eternal stream as God's desire for us and for all creation? If this is so, then the apparently incurable discontent we experience when our desires remain unfulfilled could be a divine—as well as a human—discontent.

Can discontent be divine? Perhaps it depends on whether that discontent is focused on our deepest desires or whether it has settled more superficially on our lesser wants and wishes. I am discontented when it rains on my day off or when the mail carrier doesn't bring the letter I was hoping for. This is little more than petulance. I am discontented when an important relationship goes wrong. This is disappointment and regret. But divine discontent seems to be something quite different — something even positive. It is what spurs me on to make the very best use of the gifts I have, or to go to extreme lengths to be close to someone who needs me. We see the evidence of divine discontent all around us: It is what makes the chick hatch and what fires the soul of the concert pianist. It is what leads us to realize, with Saint Augustine, that our soul finds no rest until it finds its rest in God.

Beyond the Lottery

Our desires may appear to be mismatched with God's desire because we easily get sidetracked by many "lesser" wants and wishes. We can name what we think we want, but it is much harder to probe beneath it and discern what lies at the roots of that wanting.

I noted these layers of wanting during a Monday-morning conversation with a friend on the commuter train. We began by exchanging lighthearted comments: "Are you still here then? Not laid off from work yet? Not won the lottery?"

My friend smiled ruefully and said that on the previous Friday she had just missed winning the "Spot the Ball" competition in her local newspaper. She bewailed the fact that she had won just five pounds and so narrowly missed winning two hundred thousand pounds.

I commiserated with her. Then, more out of idle curiosity than anything else, I asked her what she would have done with the two hundred thousand pounds if she had won it. At that point there was a noticeable change in the nature of the conversation. The banter was set aside, and she became quite thoughtful. We sat for a moment in silence. Then she told me that she would have bought a house with the prize money. After a few more moments, she revealed that she would have bought a big house with a garden, in Birmingham. She was obviously imagining this dream home even as she spoke. Then came the crunch, in just a few words that came straight from her heart: "I'd take my mother back there to her roots, to a nice home in the place where she grew up, the only place she really longs to be!"

Perhaps you can see, in this example, how deep the question "What are you looking for?" can go. For my friend, it could have been answered at several different levels: "I want to win a lot of money"; "I want a big house"; "I want to live in Birmingham." But underneath all of these, and much more muted, were longings that even she had not yet discovered: "I want to make my mother happy before she dies. We are longing to go back to our roots." I don't know whether she thought any more about this conversation. If she did, she might have understood something of how our deepest desires affect and drive us. Even the desire to win the lottery, though it can be dismissed as a materialistic whim, is often the tip of a hidden iceberg. What does that iceberg contain? It is well worth doing a little deep-sea diving to find out, and prayer gives us the perfect place to do just that. The exercises at the end of this chapter suggest ways of investigating both our long-term and our more immediate desires in prayer.

Too Hot to Handle?

Another common reason we hesitate to express the deepest desires of our hearts, even in the silence and secrecy of prayer, is that we think they are desires we ought not to have. Perhaps what we desire is something quite illicit. Maybe we *do* covet our neighbor's ox and ass and husband! Maybe we *do* wish our boss would meet with a fatal accident! To desire such things is by no means the same as bringing them about! Feelings are not right or wrong in themselves. It is what we do about those feelings, how we turn them into action, that makes them morally loaded.

This is not to say that such extreme feelings can be expressed easily, even to our closest friends. In fact, we often find it difficult to express such feelings to God in prayer. But there is no theological or rational reason we can't or shouldn't "take it to the Lord in prayer." Telling God our "bad" desires won't harm God, and it helps us to express to ourselves what we're feeling and to acknowledge, in humility and honesty, the power of such desires.

Perhaps we cannot express them, even in our prayer, because our image of God is punitive. Is God the judge, the policeman, the angry father or avenging lover, waiting to find a moral weakness in us? If you do find that you hit a block when trying to express such deep and possibly painful desires in prayer, try asking yourself what images you have of God and whether these images are helping you draw closer to or keeping you at a distance from him. And remember that when you do express such desires to God, you are not asking God to fulfill them, but you are simply bringing yourself to God, just as you are, and opening up in his presence. You can safely leave it to God to guide you through your inner minefields in ways that will strengthen your trust in him and in yourself.

Claiming the Energy

Did you know that there is energy locked up in your desires? Just as electric power flows from the negative to the positive poles, so too there is energy that seems to flow between where we are and where we desire to be. That gap between our desires and their fulfillment is a creative gap. Feelings of love, for example, generate the power to do things we never imagined we could do. Feelings of compassion can produce stamina and fortitude to go to extreme lengths for another person. And feelings of anger can produce the energy and courage to confront and oppose situations that are harming ourselves or others.

This energy is ours for the claiming. And we can claim it by facing our deepest longings and desires (whether they appear to be good or bad) with trust and integrity. When we make a practice in our prayer (and at other times) of noticing and naming what we are really looking for, we learn to recognize our true desires. And we discover that those true longings are the same — or at least very close to — God's desires for us.

So this becomes a valid — indeed a crucial — question in prayer: What am I really asking for? Am I asking God to attend to my petulant complaints and arrange the world and its climate around my wishes? Am I asking God to wave a magic wand over my life's disappointments and regrets? Or am I asking God to enter the deepest layers of my personality and grow me into the person I really am, the person God has created me to become?

If this third option is our choice, we will surely experience divine discontent in all our moments until God's dream of us is fulfilled. And — perhaps the greater grace — our own desiring will be moving toward complete harmony with God's grand Desire for our lives. Our will and God's will — one.

Not What, but Whom

Saint John's Gospel ends with a question similar to the one with which it begins. This time the question, asked by the risen Jesus, is addressed to Mary of Magdala. Those first disciples in John 1 had been setting out on their quest for the Lord. Mary thinks she has come to the end of her quest. The disciples had just discovered Jesus. Mary has just lost him. The disciples still had everything before them. She feels that there is nothing but grief and emptiness ahead of her. And into this terrible emptiness, Jesus speaks his question, slightly changed, again: "Who are you looking for?" (John 20:14–15).

And this, I believe, is the pattern of our desiring. It begins with our many "whats." Our little wants and wishes, our bigger hopes and dreams, our deep and sometimes hidden desires. And we go down and down, deeper into their roots. We follow Jesus' invitation to "come and see," to find out who we really are. At the end of our searching, we come to the place where, it seems, we first began. The difference is, we know now that we are no longer looking for the "what" but the "whom." When we look into the real heart of our desires, we find that what we want is to be truly and fully ourselves and to be one with God and with one another.

TAKING IT FURTHER

Streams of our desires

I was on holiday one summer in the Spanish Pyrenees. It wasn't easy to find a place to stay, but eventually we found a room for a few nights in a small village at the edge of a spectacular national park. It was an ideal spot except for the fact that there was a hydroelectric power station outside the window, and the days and nights were alive with the throbbing of its generators.

We spent a few marvelous days exploring the wild mountainous tracts of the national park. Most of all I remember the joy of finding a tiny mountain stream flowing from a spring high among the peaks. What an adventure trying to follow its course, right down to the valley. Sometimes it would show itself in little rushes of clear water or cool, bright pools, reflecting the brilliance of the skies and giving life to a carpet of mountain flowers. Then it would disappear, leaving only the slightest hint of a river that had gone underground and now rolled on unseen. And again it would reappear, perhaps as a little waterfall or a more dignified channel of deepening water. Then it would be gone again, perhaps for miles, leaving us guessing as to which direction it might have chosen. It felt as though that stream was playing games with us. Now you see it, now you don't. It had a life and an energy all its own, sometimes gentle as a kitten, sometimes majestic. It was only as I lay in bed at night, listening to the rumble of the generators, that I realized that the playful, hideaway stream held in its elusive waters the power to bring heat and light and energy to an entire human community.

I tell you this story because it was a powerful picture for me of the stream of my desiring. Perhaps you can name some of your own deep desires that find expression in such waters.

- Do you see any desires that bubble up in your life, obvious and visible, perhaps delighting you with their promise and their hope?

- Do you see any that frighten you by appearing as precipitous waterfalls that could throw you onto dangerous rocks?

- Do you sense desires that remain stubbornly out of sight, refusing to be acknowledged?

- Can you name any *particular* desires you hold in your heart that come into any of these categories? Be specific — not just

"I want to fulfill my potential" but "I want to study astrophysics and get a job at NASA."

Now, in your imagination, go down to the village at the foot of the mountain. Listen to the throb of the generators. Notice each house, lit and warmed by electricity. And let yourself simply become aware of that unbroken stream of your own deep desire, which is energizing your life in the same way.

Read cold, on a printed page, this suggestion may sound implausible. I simply urge you to *try* to get in touch with your true desires, because this is the only way to discover what energy they are releasing in your life.

Name your hopes

To notice your more immediate desires, try starting each day with just a few moments' reflection on what you are hoping for in the coming twenty-four hours. Again, be specific. And try delving down a little to the real roots of these desires.

Once you feel more comfortable with this habit of focusing on what you are hoping for day by day, try applying the same technique when you begin a period of prayer. What hopes and wishes are you bringing to the prayer? Imagine Jesus sitting with you in your sacred space, asking you (very lovingly), "What are you looking for, *today?* What would you like me to do for you?"

Revealing questions

I've found that these two questions are good for helping us see our true desires.

- Suppose you were to win a large sum of money. (Let's say a million dollars.) What would you do with it? What do your reflections on this question show you about where your deeper desires lie?

- If you were told tomorrow that you have only three months left to live, how would you spend that time?

ADDITIONAL READING

For more help in identifying the deep roots of the desires in your heart, how the many conflicts among various desires are resolved, and the whole subject of the relationship between our desires and God's will, see my book *Inner Compass* (Chicago: Loyola Press, 1999).

See also:

What Do I Want in Prayer? by William A. Barry, S.J. (Mahwah, N.J.: Paulist Press, 1994).

Befriending Our Desires, by Philip Sheldrake, S.J. (London: Darton, Longman, & Todd, 1994).

PART TWO

Learning to Focus

In part 1, I addressed ways to approach prayer. We explored the habit of cultivating inner stillness and allowing ourselves to sink "ten feet down" to a state in which our hearts are ready to become aware of and receive God, who is always with us. We also covered the need for reflection and review, to notice the real and specific ways in which our prayer connects to our daily experience, and to notice the movements of our own desires.

Once we have reached this inner stillness and established the practice of reflection, we can focus our prayer in particular ways. There are as many ways of doing this as there are people seeking God in prayer. These chapters suggest just a few.

6

Exploring Our Inner Space

The flat above the shop

God is everywhere and in everything. As you search for him, never forget that he is also searching for you.
— WILLIAM JOHNSTON, *BEING IN LOVE* —
THE PRACTICE OF CHRISTIAN PRAYER

"Who do you think you are?" The words might sound aggressive, but discovering the answer to the question, bit by bit, day by day, is the most thrilling and rewarding venture of life.

Not far from my home there is a little shop that sells electrical goods. I'm fascinated by this place, because it gives me a clue in the search for who I am. The shop is the ground floor of a three-story house. It has a big display window that shows the goods on sale, the special offers, price lists, opening times, and so on. The sign tells you what the shop is there for. It doesn't tell you anything about the shopkeeper.

The floor above the shop is where the family lives. Its windows are smaller and covered with net curtains. This is the private place for the family, open somewhat to the world outside but much more shielded and certainly not "open all hours." You might go in there and feel quite at ease, but only if you knew the family or were invited there as a friend.

Then at the top of the house is the gable space, a third story high above the main road. This is probably a small bedroom or a study or a child's play room. The window is tiny. The person in the room can look out of it, but no one can look in, so it doesn't need elaborate curtains. You could look down onto the road from this window, but from this third story your eyes would more likely look upwards; up there it is halfway to heaven! And what fascinates me especially about this top story is that there are two initials engraved above the window, just below the roof. Presumably these are the initials of the first owner, but to the casual passerby they must always remain a mystery.

Why does this place intrigue me so much? I think it is because it reminds me of my own life. I also have three stories. There is the ground-floor me, where I do my job and join my clubs and align myself with this or that good cause or interest group. My "shop part" shows only my public self, and it opens up to the public for as long and as often as I think necessary to keep the bread on my table and remain a reasonably social individual. You can look in my shop window and deduce quite a bit about the kind of person I am and how I am different from other people. But at the end of the day, you still won't know much about the real me.

But if you could go upstairs to the second story, you would discover a lot more clues — who my friends are, what family I have, what colors I like, what books I read, and whether you feel at ease with me or not.

And were you to be invited right up to the top of my house, you might glimpse the innermost reality of me that only God can fully know. That is where my initials are stamped — the name that God will give me for eternity — and that is a mystery to me as well as to you.

This house is only a metaphor, but if it appeals to you, you might like to think about your own house, maybe even draw a picture of it. What is in your shop window? What is your public self about? What are your opening hours? Are you on demand to your public too much? Or too little? Are the customers draining you or enriching you? Do you think your shop is doing well, or are you feeling close to bankruptcy? Do you ever wish your shop were in some different trade? These are just a few questions to encourage you to notice the ground floor of your life and how you feel about it.

Now go upstairs and explore your living quarters. How are things up there? How is the family? Is the room lonely or packed with friends? What do you find there about yourself and your preferences and interests? How at ease do you feel about sharing this part of your house? Is there anyone you feel you need to exclude from it, or anyone you long to invite in but feel you can't?

Finally, climb the winding staircase up to your little attic. How would you describe this innermost, secret space inside you? Does it feel peaceful or turbulent right now? Look around this room. When you reflect on what it contains, would you feel comfortable about inviting a close friend into it or not? Is there anything you would want to put away in a cupboard first? Do you share this room, ever, with another human being? How does the atmosphere feel in this room: warm, accepting, welcoming, reproachful, frightening, imprisoning or liberating, suffocating or life-giving?

The Walled Garden

Maybe houses are not for you. Maybe you see your inner world more like a garden. A favorite place of mine is an island off the northeast coast of Britain. The first thing you would notice, if you landed on this or any other island, would be the harbor and the beaches fringing the island's coastline. If you had the time to explore it more extensively, you would find the fields and forests farther inland, where the islanders grow their crops and cultivate their trees and keep their animals. On my particular island, however, there is also a small but very lovely castle, and close to the castle is a tiny walled garden, which is accessible only at certain times when the gardener is in. This garden is lovingly tended, and it blooms with a variety of herbs and blossoms. It was originally planted by the owners of the castle, who wanted it to be a special place that would express their personal delight in life and provide peace and solitude—a place where they could be themselves, away from their public image.

Again, I see myself—my inner spaces—in parallels with this island. I find aspects of myself that I might call the harbors and landing stages of my life within the human family. These are places where I meet people and let them into my life — or keep them out! I find a whole outer fringe of me — my beaches, where I am in direct contact, minute by minute, with the turbulent, demanding, unpredictable world around me. Then I move inland, where I can discover the what and how of my existence. What is my work about? What crops am I growing? What am I best at? What am I bad at? Where are the wild, overgrown areas of my life, and where are my fields in better order? In what part of my island do I feel most at home and comfortable? Where do I feel threatened?

And then we come to the walled garden. This is like the top story of the house. It is my innermost space where I meet with God and to which only a few other human hearts have access. What grows in that garden? God has planted it for his own delight and for mine and ultimately for the delight of all who dwell in his kingdom. When I spend time in that walled garden, I am being invited to discover just who *God* thinks I am!

Another garden that always refreshes and inspires me is nestled in the heart of Chester Cathedral. This cathedral image, if it isn't too overwhelming, can also be a route to the heart of ourselves. The cathedral stands visible and obvious in its neighborhood. Like us, it is physically there, present to the world around it. Inside you'll find a vast public space, open alike to tourists and worshipers. And our inner space too is partially open to all those with whom we interact. To go deeper inside the cathedral, at Chester at least, you have to take a little trouble to find your way into the cloisters. This is a private, prayerful place, less frequented, more meaningful and reflective. Here it is possible to stroll quietly, to "circle the center," to be closer to the heartbeat that holds us in being. And as you walk around the cloisters, you will notice a little wooden door with a latch. Sometimes it is locked. But if you are lucky and the door opens for you, you find yourself on the threshold of a small, secluded garden with a fountain at its center. Here is the secret space of your meeting point with God, and it is fed by the spring of living water that God is opening up in your heart.

Growing Where You Are Planted

"If only I could have my life again, be born into a different family, choose a different job, a different lifestyle, begin again, knowing what I know now . . ."

Almost everyone indulges in this daydream from time to time. When I feel these thoughts coming on, a short respite in my innermost garden helps me see things rather differently. For instance, sometimes "spring bulbs" tell me their story — of being buried beneath a suffocating weight of the clay. There in the clay it is cold, wet, dark, and lonely. But that same deadening clay is the provider of the bulbs' nutrition all through the unobserved growing months. From them I see that the circumstance we so often long to escape is the very place, and the *only* place, that can provide the means of our growth and bring us to the moment of rebirth in due season.

And next time you have a chance to do so, try holding a seed in your hand — any seed will do. If you drop that seed into the ground it will, in its own good time, become whatever it is destined to be. When that time comes, you might like to reflect on a simple equation: The seed plus the soil equals the flower.

The soil — that cloying weight of unchangeable circumstances in which you live out your life — is the added ingredient that turns the seed into the flower. In fact, the flower is *made* of that soil. The loveliest, most fragrant blossom at the flower show is *made* of soil! But that soil has been transfigured and transformed by the hidden reality of the seed that is doing its silent becoming down in the earth. Small wonder that Jesus invited us to "consider the lilies of the field" (Matthew 6:28 KJV). They have a key to wisdom that we, perhaps, lost when we first left the Garden.

❧ TAKING IT FURTHER ❧

Into the house

A helpful exercise might be to invite God to come with you into your house and just show him around, starting at the ground floor and working up. When you have finished your tour, change roles with God for a few minutes, and ask *God* to guide *you* around, starting at the top, where you and God are closest, and working down to street level. You can ask God to show you how what happens in the attic filters its way down through the family quarters, to the shop, and out into the street.

Go to the island

In your imagination, take a boat out to your island and spend some time exploring it. Explore its beaches and its landing stages. Go inland and see what is growing there and what your island is all about. Finally, ask God to unlock the gate to your walled garden and take you inside. Ask God to introduce you to the flowers and shrubs and herbs growing there, to tell you how much he enjoys planting and tending them, and to share with you all that he hopes they will become. Simply share in his delight. Let this sanctuary of joy become a place to return to when you are struggling with all the problems in the surrounding fields and even out beyond the island.

Think about your soil

If you can imagine yourself as a seed or a spring bulb buried deep in the winter earth, try to become aware of the nature of the soil in which you are planted — the soil of your personal circumstances. How does this soil feel on the whole? Light, heavy, supportive, oppressive, nourishing or draining? Just reflect on it for a few minutes and see what descriptions come to mind. These are your real feelings about your circumstances, coming to the surface of your mind to claim your attention. Don't suppress them or judge them. They are pointers to your deepest self.

Now look back over the years of your life. Imagine that now is your heart's "spring." Your seed or bulb has broken through the soil to blossom in the May sunshine. From where has it drawn its food and water for this miraculous becoming? Can you name any particular aspects of your circumstances that have provided that food and water, even though it may not have felt like that at the time?

7

Praying Our Stories

Your history — your mystery

⁂

The whole Hebrew Bible is a story of human tragedies,
but when these tragedies are lived and remembered
as the context in which God's unconditional love for
the people of Israel is revealed, this story becomes
sacred history.

— HENRI NOUWEN, *SABBATICAL JOURNEY*

Using the stilling and relaxing skills we looked at in chapter 3, let's spend a few moments listening to a *story*. Read the following two paragraphs, and see which one of them speaks to you. Don't bother about their content. Just notice your gut reaction to what you are reading. For example, is it boring or interesting, meaningful to you or just something you will forget as soon as you have read it?

During the years 1945 to 1989, East Germany was a separate state under Soviet occupation. It was ruled by a communist puppet government. By 1961 so many people were fleeing to the West that the authorities closed the borders and built the infamous Berlin Wall to prevent people going from East to West. Young people hoping to enter higher education were required to join the Communist Party. It was a grave crime to try to leave East Germany for a western country, and many refugees were killed in the attempt. In November 1989, in an uprising of all the communist totalitarian countries of Eastern Europe, the Soviet stranglehold was broken. In Berlin the uprising led to the breaching of the Berlin

Wall on November 9, and the reunification of East and West Germany followed in 1990.

Now listen to a rather different way of looking at these facts of history:

> Peter was born in the middle of the War, in the eastern part of Berlin. He remembers bombers howling overhead and his parents carrying him to air raid shelters. When he was nineteen, Peter realized he wasn't going to be allowed to stay at university unless he joined the Communist Party. Events speeded up dramatically at that time, and he was confronted by a snap decision. On August 12, 1961, he heard rumors that something was about to happen along the borders. Peter took his chance and, with nothing more than his swimming trunks, he swam across the Teltow Canal and asked for political asylum in the West. The next day the borders to East Berlin were closed behind him, and it would be nineteen years before he saw his mother again. His cousin, Konrad, stayed behind in the East. But he too was destined to cross the border in a dramatic way. On November 9, 1989, East Berlin was again buzzing with rumor: Something was happening along the borders. Konrad went off to see what was going on. When he arrived at the Wall, he couldn't believe his eyes. Half of Berlin seemed to have gathered there. People were going across to the West! The border was open! The guards stood there bemused, not knowing what to do about it. Konrad drove from East to West Berlin in his old Trabi, and someone poured a bottle of champagne over the car as he drove through the open checkpoint. The two cousins met up again soon afterwards — an emotional reunion. They hugged each other in silence, both too choked up to speak. Their story was history!

Again: Which of these two accounts of postwar life in Germany do you relate to more? Which one is more likely to stick in your memory?

Jesus habitually used stories to teach us about the kingdom. If you read the Gospels, you will find whole books full of stories. And what kind of theology do we relate to more easily? The theology that spells out the moral principles and the theories of redemption that underlie our faith or the story that begins: "There was once a carpenter's son in Nazareth . . ."?

I would suggest that the beginning—and the whole purpose—of our continuing relationship with God lies in our *story*. The meaning and destination of our lives lie in the way *our story* connects to Jesus and the *gospel story* of redemption.

So I would like to invite you to reflect on your story, because that is, I believe, where you will most easily find the traces of God's action in your life.

Tracing Your Story

When our daughter was in elementary school, she was given an exercise to plot the family history as far as she could. We had information about her ancestors in two strands of the family (one German and one Scottish), going back for about two hundred years, so we helped her explore this project by drawing a time line. On one side of the line, we marked the main events in world history (such as the invention of electricity and the automobile) and in European history especially (such as the World Wars and the building of the Berlin Wall). On the other side of the time line, we marked significant events in the family, including the births and deaths of all the family members we could trace. Now, as I look back, I see a significant value in connecting our family story with the world story. I see how helpful it can be to connect the outward and obvious facts of our lives with the underlying movements in our hearts that reveal to us where God is for us and how he is forming us.

You might like to try this as an exercise in prayer. Begin by making a note of the important events in your life: your birth, your start to school, changes of school, college days, jobs, important relationships, marriage, the birth of children, of grandchildren, the names of friends, places you have lived, holidays you especially remember, and so on. You could call this the *visible* side of your time line.

So far so good. Now turn to the *invisible* side of your story—those things that no outside observer would notice but that may turn out to be the most significant things of all. For this part of the exercise, ask God to open the eyes of your heart to see where the most life-giving and life-changing points in your story have been. This is an exercise in prayer. Don't try to force your own memory but turn to God's grace and trust him to bring you to an awareness of what he is inviting you to remember.

Some examples of these inner landmarks might be: events or encounters that caused some change of heart and made you see things from a different perspective; moments when perhaps the world stood still for you, and you felt touched by God; times of particular darkness when you felt abandoned by God; seasons during which wise people have profoundly influenced your inner journey.

How have any life-giving moments made a difference to you since they happened? And those events that seemed destructive at the time — have they actually destroyed you? With hindsight, can you see any way in which these dark patches of your experience have led you to new growth spurts? Which experiences do you most relish — and which do you most regret? Let them both be there, simply laid bare before God in your prayer. Don't try to suppress the feelings you may have about them. Let your joy be expressed. Let your tears be shed. This kind of prayer is an intimate encounter with the Lord; let it renew your energy.

These landmarks of your life are a map of the way God is bringing you, mile by mile, to the fullness of your life in him. As you recall and reflect, notice times of learning from him; times of comfort, like a child hiding in his arms; times when you have turned away and tried to go it alone; times when conflict has driven you fear-filled back to his presence; times when he seemed utterly distant. Notice decisive crossroads and significant encounters, periods of stagnation and spurts of growth.

If you were to read the Old Testament as a map of the story of the redemption of all humanity, you would find in it your own story writ large. You too have known the joys of the first paradise and the pain of alienation from your true self. You have likely known personal captivities, spent seasons in the desert, made your own exodus, crossed to a promised land. You have learned the rules of what it means to be disciplined and the grace of what it means to be loved. You have lamented and rejoiced, been faithful and unfaithful. You have trusted, doubted, rebelled, but kept on going. You are one with all this community of humanity and called into this communion with God.

Everything you have experienced in your search for God and for meaning is recorded there in the struggles and the triumphs of the people of Israel — and of the whole human family.

When you see your personal story as being connected with the whole human story of redemption, you are coming close to the heart of the meaning of your life. You are discovering that that meaning is part of the meaning of all God's creation. Like the two cousins in Berlin, your story becomes linked to another person's story — *his*-story, and his story of creation and redemption holds *your* story.

A Patchwork Quilt

Another memory from our daughter's school days is the gift the school gave to the principal when she retired. A few months before the retirement date, the teachers asked all the students to make a little patch and embroider their own name on it. The patches were then collected and sewn together to make a quilt for the loved and respected principal. The children threw themselves into the task with enthusiasm, and the resulting quilt was a delight to them all. It included a little bit of every child, and it brought the principal to tears when she saw it. When she would look at it, every patch would bring to life again a child she had cherished in her own particular way. And the whole quilt, made up of her memories, would keep her warm in the years ahead.

A good way to get in touch with your story is to collect your own "patches." A patch can be whatever comes to your mind as you reflect back over the story of your life: special moments and significant relationships; journeys you have made; turning points; memorable places; regrets and sorrows; joys and enthusiasms. You can "collect" them in practical ways, for example by writing down your thoughts about significant moments in your life, or by browsing picture albums or scrapbooks. Or you can "collect" them inwardly, simply by registering them in your heart, as you recall them in prayer, and welcoming them into your memory. (You might like to do this more systematically, in the form of a prayer journal, as suggested in chapter 24).

Anything and everything might turn up among your patches. And all together they can represent a *wholeness* that is *you*. Your story is like the quilt that comes into being when your patches come together. It is absolutely unique and crammed full of meaning and a beauty all its own. If that principal dissolved into tears of joy when she saw her pupils' gift, how do you think God is going to respond when you bring him the poignant patchwork of your life?

The quilt is about wholeness, the coming together of all that is you to make something that is greater than the sum of its parts. And that new quilt that is your life in its wholeness is not just for yourself. It is becoming a quilt for the warming and holding of others.

Your story is God's story, lived out in you, and it is also *our* story, the story of the whole human family, which cannot be complete until your part of it is told and celebrated.

❧ TAKING IT FURTHER ❧

Remember your life

During the next few days or weeks, try to take a little time in prayer just to remember your life and the making of your faith story so far. There are many ways to do this. Two are suggested here, but you may prefer to find your own way of recalling memorable, life-changing people, events, conversations, meetings, and experiences.

- Imagine your life as a mountain pathway you've climbed. What crags does the path run through? What special views along the way have left you with a sense of joy and wonder? What signposts have been helpful to you? What major milestones have you passed, and how do you feel about them? What important discoveries have been along the path? Where did the path begin, and where is it leading you? What baggage are you carrying, and do you ever wish it were not so heavy? Which companions have been alongside you at different times, as you have been walking your path? What landmarks have guided you on your journey?

• We believe, as Christians, that Jesus walks alongside us on our life's path. But does this truth mean anything to us in practice? In the Gospel we find a journey made by two people very much like ourselves. They are walking to the village of Emmaus, not far from Jerusalem, after the events of Good Friday, and they are feeling about as low as a person can feel. They had pinned all their hopes on Jesus as the Messiah, and now he has been put to death as a common criminal. The sense of disillusionment and despair overwhelms them. Then a stranger comes alongside them, and they fall into conversation with him. He appears to be the only person around who hasn't heard about the events of the Passover in Jerusalem. But he notices their despair, and he gently draws them to trust him and share their story with him. Imagine that you are one of those travelers. Let the gentle stranger come up beside you and draw you into conversation. He asks about your story and why you are making this journey. He asks how you feel about the events of your own life's story, and how you are feeling now. Tell him in your prayer. Don't be afraid to show him your negative feelings as well as the happier memories. After a while you come to a crossroads. The stranger appears to be going straight on, but night is falling and you need to stop over in the inn. How do you feel about your walk with the stranger? What happens next in your imagination? You will find this story in Luke 24:13 – 35.

8

Reviewing the Day with God

Action replay

✳

*Our treasure lies hidden in the field of our experience
and in the inner life which results from that experience.*
— GERARD HUGHES, *GOD OF SURPRISES*

For about nine months recently, I was visiting a sick friend and his wife each week to take them Holy Communion. The man was dying of cancer, and his wife was looking after him and making this last journey in faith alongside him, knowing that very soon they would be parted. He died just a few weeks before their golden wedding anniversary.

Although it was harrowing in many ways to see these friends every week facing the anguish of impending loss, facing death and all its fears, I looked forward to these weekly visits. When I arrived, the three of us would sit down together after we had received the Sacrament. My friend would invariably say, "Let's tell Margaret about the things that have been really good during this week." And I would sit and listen as they recounted a story of someone who had visited and brought them a piece of news or a new insight or perspective on the world, or maybe one of them had been reading something that moved him or her.

Nearly every week I left with a book they had lent me or a poem or an article they had photocopied for me to read. Perhaps they would have received a letter. Or maybe a new flower had come out in the garden. Or they had spotted a visiting bird. Often

59

the good thing of that week was a flash of memory that one of them had experienced or a dream that had left them feeling calm and at peace or simply an act of kindness—a neighbor had called, a son or daughter had phoned, the nurse had been gentle, the mailman had told a joke. Then they would turn to me and ask about *my* week and invite me to share my remembered treasure.

In these months I began to see that it was possible, whatever the outward circumstances, to discover a golden thread that stood out and brightened the fabric of each day. There might be only one thing that shone out with that sparkle, but there *would* be one thing, if we opened our eyes to see, that was definitely worth searching for. It was a gift from God. And I know now, looking back on that time, that this approach to the presence of God in my friends' daily lives was changing those months from what might have been a time of agony, despair, and self-pity into a time of amazing, out-flowing awareness and joy.

In the previous chapter, we considered our personal life story and where God has been in it. Now I invite you to bring the focus in a bit closer and try reviewing the day, or perhaps the week, in the same kind of way, with an eye constantly open to spot the golden thread that sparkled in the day's fabric. The practice of reviewing the day prayerfully with God has come down to us through countless generations of Christians. There is nothing new or revolutionary about it. In this prayer you are in the company of millions of Christians from across the centuries. But it *could* cause a revolution in your way of looking at your ordinary, everyday life.

Color Your Day

Having recognized a golden thread in your day (or in your week, if that is easier for you at first), you might like to try filling in some of the other colors that have been around for you. Your passing moods may help you with this. As you look back over the day and replay its events and encounters, try to notice how you were feeling.

- What were the main moods of your day?

- What elated you? What left you feeling disappointed or down?

- What made you angry?

- Did anything give rise to a surge of joy inside you?

Can you identify where the roots of these feelings may lie? For example, a feeling of unease or distress around a particular event in your day may be revealing some unfinished business or some damaged relationship that you subconsciously sense you need to attend to. If so, lay it before God honestly, ask for his healing, and listen to whatever suggestions arise in your heart. They may be showing you a new way forward in dealing with the problem.

Or moods of elation may be pointing to aspects of your life that are helping you grow and nourishing a sense of joy and genuine well-being. Notice these moods and try to follow them to their deeper roots. Let them lead you down to the sources of what is life-giving in your day-by-day experience. Thank God for these things in your life and ask God to help you draw on them more and more, so that they may become increasingly life-giving for you and those around you — your family, friends, colleagues, and neighbors.

Are There Any Dark Patches?

When I visited my dying friend, I knew perfectly well that he would have experienced times of darkness in his week. It would have been dishonest to pretend that the whole week had been one long, golden thread. Now, as I look back to those visits, I realize that the darkness used to be expressed as we received the Sacrament itself, as we prayed together and asked God for his healing touch on whatever had been out of order, in ourselves or in the world around us, during the week. At those times nobody needed to say very much aloud about the darkness experienced in his or her heart. We would just express in simple terms any feeling of pain, fear, guilt, or inadequacy we recalled from the week. Nobody would make any comment. The dark patch would be received and acknowledged in a loving silence between us and laid before God.

As you look back over the day, you may notice incidents in which you feel that you failed to respond to God's love or to another person's needs. Tell God how you feel. Ask God to shine the light of his love in those particular places, even though that light may hurt your eyes and make you cry. Trust that God will enlighten your darkness with gentleness and love. Express sorrow for anything that still grieves you, and ask for the grace to begin again tomorrow with a lightened heart and renewed courage.

If you make this action-replay prayer at the end of the day, end it by committing yourself, and all those you love, into God's care, as a child might fall asleep in a mother's arms.

If All Else Fails

Let me make two suggestions for staying close to God in prayer, even — and especially — when you feel unable to pray or it has been one of those days when all you want to do is forget about it and fall asleep.

We all experience times when prayer feels quite out of reach. If you find yourself in a phase like this and you have no time or inclination for any other kind of prayer, try to spend a few minutes before you fall asleep replaying the main events and feelings of your day, as you might rerun a video in fast forward until something catches your attention and you slow the action down to view it more carefully. Just notice those moments that grab you and hold them, in your memory and before God.

This kind of prayer, which many call the review of the day (you may also find it called the *examen* or the review of consciousness), has the power to touch the whole of your day with your unspoken desire to discover God's presence in it. You will find that it soon becomes a habit that will increase your awareness of God's presence in your whole life.

If you don't have the time or the energy to replay your whole day like this, try noticing just one thing for which you would like to

say "thank you" to God. I remember going to work one morning—
to an office in a desolate and rundown place in Manchester. I was
feeling depressed and dreading the day ahead. As I walked from
the station through the grim back streets and past half-demolished
buildings, my physical surroundings seemed to echo my own
mood. Then all at once, as I walked along, head down, hoping
not to be mugged, I noticed a glorious clump of clover blooming
triumphantly in the rubble and a huge bumblebee gathering nec-
tar from it—here in this, the most unpromising place. That was
my "just one thing" to thank God for that day, and I have never
forgotten that somehow, somewhere, there is always a clump of
clover in the rubble, if we open our eyes to see as God sees.

❈ TAKING IT FURTHER ❈

Pick up the phone

To help you feel comfortable with review-the-day prayer, you
might try this imaginative exercise.

Find a comfortable place to sit. Close your eyes or focus your
gaze, perhaps on a candle. Relax and let the tensions of the day
slip away for a few minutes.

The day has been . . . how *has* the day been? There may have
been problems to resolve, surprises to rejoice over, encounters to
remember. Or perhaps there is only the aching loneliness of a day
without human contact or human hope.

Then the silence is broken. The phone rings. Imagine picking up
the phone—with excitement, with irritation?—and hearing a
warm, concerned voice: "I just called to ask how your day has
been. Tell me about it. Tell me how you are. Tell me how you feel."

Take the phone to your favorite chair. Settle yourself for this
most welcome of calls. Curl up and relax. The call is free. You can
talk for as long as you like.

Begin by savoring the fact that a friend has called you. "I'm
so glad that we have this time together," he tells you. It occurs to
you that, though he is your closest friend, you have scarcely given

him a thought all day. But *he* has not forgotten you, and he is here to tell you just that.

How does the conversation go? You might first bring to mind the blessings of the day. What has happened to make you want to thank him? Has there been a meeting with someone or a letter or a friendly, unexpected word or gesture? Has anything made you laugh? Have you solved some problem? Have you noticed something good in the world around you—a lovely sunset, a refreshing shower for the garden, a momentary break in the cloud cover that revealed a patch of blue sky?

Remember those who have deserved your gratitude today. Those who grew the food you have eaten, those who picked the leaves for the tea you have drunk. Those who have done something for you that they didn't need to do. And finally—and you may not find this easy—remember something about yourself and your day that you can be proud about. Then hear your friend's voice saying, "Well done!"

These are the raw materials of your prayer. Ask God—your friend—to help you to see how his love for you has been working in these facts and these feelings.

Now reflect on what you have recalled, trusting that the awareness of God's action in your day has been given. Notice, for example:

- What has drawn you closer to God today?

- What have you learned about God and about the way God's kingdom works?

- What happened to make you feel loved today? And were you able to give a sign of love to another person?

- What kind of moods were present in your day? Just notice them, without any judgment.

- It's OK to tell God about how angry you were with the neighbor, how impatient with the children, how moved by some unexpected offer of help, how helpless in the face of some suffering. It's OK to tell God that the day has been unspeakably awful and that all you can say for it is that you are glad it's over.

Is there any unfinished business that you would like to raise—has anything left you feeling inadequate or displeased with yourself or with someone else or fearful for the consequences still to come?

Simply express whatever is in your heart, in whatever way feels right for you. Say as much or as little as you like, because in the end this conversation isn't about words. It is a heart-to-heart encounter.

Before you put the phone down, spend a few moments looking forward to tomorrow. Ask your friend to open your eyes and ears to see and notice everything he wants to reveal to you of himself in its hours and its events. Ask your friend to make you alert to his surprises and to his presence in everyone you will meet.

And be sure, before you end the conversation, to hear your friend's words of blessing: "Goodnight, my dear. I love you. I bless you. Sleep in peace."

9

Praying for Others

"With love and prayers . . ."

※

Go-between God:
inweave the fabric of our common life,
that the many-coloured beauty of your love
may find expression in all our exchanges.

— Jennifer Wild, in the
SPCK Book of Christian Prayer

Do you ever end a letter with these or similar words? I often do it myself. And I mean what I say. I really mean that I will be holding that person in my prayer. But what, if anything, do I mean by that? What good do my prayers do for the person I am writing to? Does my promise to pray offer anything more than a warm feeling that someone is thinking of him or her? This is no bad thing in itself, but is it *prayer?*

I have struggled greatly with this problem through the years and seriously wondered what intercessory prayer can mean in the presence of a God who knows the needs of those we pray for far better than we ever could. We can reel off a list of names and requests like a checklist that may leave us feeling satisfied that we have prayed for the people on the list. But have we actually done anything at all? And what more than prayer could we do?

Journeying to the Center

To make some sense of intercessory prayer, I envision a picture of the human family: All of humanity make up the circumference of a vast circle. Each of us has a place on this circumference, just as we have a place on the surface of the earth. We feel close to people who seem to be in the same place as we are, and we feel diametrically opposed to others, who happen to be (in terms of their opinions, temperament, or even their spirituality) on the opposite side of the circle.

But the whole circle is centered on God, in whom it has its entire existence. God is the hub around which all of us spin. When we go into prayer, we are at the very least signaling our *desire* to be with God in that center. We discover that our own core is in some mysterious way also the center who is God. Our truest self is a particle of God's self. To pray is to bring ourselves into resonance with that universal center.

If this picture works for you, you might be able to see that when you pray for particular individuals and their needs, you are doing two things:

- You are gathering them from around the circumference of this circle (from nearby or from far away), first of all into your own thoughts. When you mention each name, you are consciously and deliberately bringing that person into your mind.

- You are then bringing yourself and those you have gathered down to the center of yourself, to the still and silent place where you know yourself to be part of — one with — God.

What happens there, in the center of things, need not concern us. A familiar scene may bring it closer: imagine, perhaps, that the year has dragged on with little letup in bad weather. It gets to August. Children are fractious and bad-tempered. Elderly relatives are pale and depressed. You would give anything for a break and a glimpse of the sun. Then the weather suddenly takes a turn for the better. The skies clear. The temperature rises. The sun smiles.

You gather your flock into the car, buckets and spades included. You collect Granddad en route and off you go to the coast.

You could have gone on your own. But it mattered to you that these other people in your life also have a season in the sun. As you relax on the beach, knowing that the children are reveling in this space of sun and sand and sea and that Granddad will relish the memory of this day through many wintry months ahead, you don't need to analyze *why* this day is good for all of them. Enough to know that it *is*.

I think something similar happens when we pray for others. We take them with us, as it were, into the radiance of God's presence, and we don't need to know why this is a good thing to do or how it may be affecting them. We just know that it *is*.

Bedrock Connections

I am fascinated by the fact that, though we see our world as a series of islands and continents set in vast ocean tracts, if we can imagine the tide going out radically and universally, we would see all our islands and continents as a single lump of rock beneath the tide line.

In the Book of Revelation, Saint John tells us that in the new heaven and the new earth there is no more sea. This may be bad news to those like me who love the sea in all its shapes and forms. But note that in the Jewish worldview, the sea was seen as the container of all that was evil or threatening. And certainly, whatever our feelings about the sea, it is what separates our islands and continents and obscures the reality of our bedrock oneness.

"No man is an island," wrote John Donne. And yet most of us live for the most part *as if we were islands*. We tend to guard and cherish our separateness from everyone else and live from a center of gravity within ourselves, rather than from the true center of gravity in the heart of our wholeness and oneness. But when we pray, the tide goes out. We shift our inner center of gravity from ourselves to God. We get a glimpse of the bedrock union in which all of us have our eternal being.

What might this mean for intercessory prayer? For me, it means that I am brought face to face with the reality that I and the woman next door, the colleague at the next desk, the drug pusher in the courtroom, and his victim in the rehab center are all made of the same stuff. We all live on that common bedrock. Although this realization doesn't change anything in the way God sees us and cares for us, it certainly changes *our* perspectives. It becomes clear that others' joy, pain, saintliness, and sinfulness are intimately, inseparably one with our own. When we pray for someone, if we do so genuinely and with a real desire to be with her, we meet her not on our terms or on her terms but on God's. The real test of such prayer is this: Will we remember how we are united when the tide comes in and we are islands again and tempted to rebuild the fences between us?

At Home with God

One thing that especially helps me to pray for others is becoming familiar with their physical surroundings. Once I know a person's home environment, or if I have been with her in a place that she loves, it becomes much easier to go there in my prayer, taking the Lord with me (or, rather, letting the Lord take me). It makes more sense of Jesus' promise that "where two or more are gathered in my name I am there in the midst of them" (Matthew 18: 20).

In my prayer space and my prayer time I can be with the one I pray for in a very real and familiar way, and I can know that the two of us are in the Lord's presence.

Taking the trouble to get to know a person on his or her home ground brings other benefits too:

- It forces me to focus more on the other person's real needs and not on my desire to be helpful on my own terms. It shifts the center of gravity to that person's place and away from my own.

- It shows in a concrete way the place, and maybe even the means, through which my prayers may be answered in practical ways. If I know the person's living space, I am much more likely to notice where her practical needs are centered.

Being at home with God starts with a call to be at home with each other.

Bringing Back God's Answers

There is a village in Derbyshire that was almost wiped out by the Bubonic Plague in 1665–66. It is famous because at that time the villagers made a deliberate, collective, and courageous decision to isolate themselves to protect the surrounding neighborhood from contagion. During this terrible time, they would collect their supplies of food, medication, and news of the outside world from the boundary stones that marked the circumference of the isolation zone.

Whenever I walk along the path between the village and one of these boundary stones, I am very moved by the memory of these people. I imagine perhaps the one remaining healthy member of a stricken family trudging along this path to collect the food and medication and letters left at the boundary stone by their benefactors from the surrounding villages. I am even more moved when I turn from the stone and retrace my steps back to the village. That one healthy person, still capable of making the life-giving journey to the boundary stone, could so easily have stayed there or slipped off into the surrounding hills to safety. But he or she turned back instead, back to the village, putrid with the smell of death, bringing back the means of life from the boundary. Back into the risk of contagion. Back to the mute suffering of the plague victims. Back to the ones who did not have the strength to help themselves.

This, for me, is what it means to pray for each other. It means that we cooperate with God in answering these prayers. It means turning our pleas into action. The plague victims in the village trusted that the means of life would indeed be brought to the boundary stones. But, being too weak themselves, they also needed someone who knew the way and had the strength to make the journey on their behalf. And they needed someone who would come back to them, however tempting it might be to stay forever with the Lord and overlook their own responsibilities in God's desire for people's salvation.

Becoming the Answer to Your Prayers

John 5:1–13 describes a scene at the Pool of Bethesda in Jerusalem. This poolside was frequented by people in dire need of healing, such as those who were blind or unable to walk. They would congregate there because there was a tradition that when the waters were stirred (by an angel it was believed), the first person to reach the pool would be healed.

Some years ago I spent considerable time listening to the story of someone who had been searching all his life for a real and personal relationship with God. Eventually he asked me to be with him in a local church during his first attempt to meet God in imaginative prayer (see chapter 16). I suggested this passage to him as a focus for his prayer, little realizing the implications it would have for both of us.

I accompanied him rather reluctantly, feeling that it would be better for him to be alone. Once there I found a quiet corner in the church, some distance away from him, and sat down to wait. It took a few minutes before it occurred to me that it might be a good thing to pray for him and with him at this significant time. At first my prayers for him were the only kind of intercessory prayer I knew. I lobbed my requests over the fence at God, asking him to do what needed to be done for this man and to give him the healing he was asking for.

Almost in spite of myself, however, I found that I too was being drawn into imaginative prayer, and where else would I go, in the circumstances, but to the Pool of Bethesda? I sat down at the poolside to wait for my friend. A patient observer? Or an observer of the patient? Then Jesus approached me, sat down beside me, and drew me into conversation.

"What do you think they are doing here?" he asked me.

That was easy. "They are waiting to be healed. When the angel stirs the water, one of them will go in and be healed."

"What is wrong with them?" Jesus continued.

"Some are blind and others are paralyzed."

"So how will any of them get to the pool when the water is stirred? Surely those who are blind won't see that the water has been stirred, and the ones who are paralyzed will see it but they won't be able to move."

The simple logic confounded me, and I had an uneasy feeling that Jesus had meant it to! He smiled with a gentle determination and said, "No one will reach the healing water alone. They all need someone who will take them. They need someone else's eyes and limbs."

This was the first time — the first of many times — when Jesus challenged me to become the answer to my own prayers of intercession. Teresa of Avila reminds us that God has no hands on earth now but ours, no eyes and no limbs but ours. If we ask God to act on behalf of others, we must be willing to become the implements of that action. Perhaps our reluctance to do so is the reason many of our intercessions seem to remain unanswered.

❈ TAKING IT FURTHER ❈

A closer look at your prayer

Cast your mind back over the past week or so. Can you name any of the people you have been praying for? You might even like to jot down their names and remind yourself of why you have been praying for them (but destroy the paper afterwards, to protect their confidentiality).

Take a few minutes to look closely at what you have been asking God to do. Maybe focus on just one or two people who are often in your prayers. What are you actually hoping God will do for those people? Is there any way you can at least make a start on the job yourself? Asking God to heal a person who suffers from chronic, debilitating depression may be asking God for a miracle that begins with a single friendly smile, a loving letter or phone call, or a generous gift of an hour out of a busy day to visit that one whose hours are like eternities. We so often hold back from making the first step because we cannot imagine where the road will lead from there.

Your "at home" group

Think of a group of people in which you feel at home. It may be a church-based group or a group with which you enjoy some hobby or sport. No doubt through the years new people have joined the group and others have gone away. Tomorrow, for all you know, a new person may come along, someone you have never seen before; before long that person may become a valued friend.

And now the exercise: Next time you are out in town, at the mall, on the road behind the steering wheel, or anywhere surrounded by strangers, notice your feelings. All too often, I feel impatient with the crowds around me and irritated when strangers slow me down or get in my way. When this happens I sometimes (I wish I could say always) try to look into one or two of the faces of these strangers and see, instead of a nuisance, the face of the person who might be the next to join my group.

For example, I sometimes help give retreats, often in parishes where I don't know anyone. When the outside world is getting on top of me on a busy Saturday morning, I sometimes stop to reflect that the next face I see might be arriving at the next parish retreat. Immediately, I see that person differently. I assume the best about him instead of the worst. I assume that he is searching for God and for meaning, that he is a person of good will, where only minutes earlier I had been looking upon him as someone whose whole aim in life was to get in front of me at the fish counter. In short, I see him, however briefly, *as he really is,* and not as an extension of my own impatience. Just a small way of meeting one another in the bedrock wholeness, perhaps, but a method that can be easily practiced, wherever we find ourselves.

10

Bringing the World's Events to God

Two column inches

※

The Kingdom is not some kind of extraterrestrial entity
that will be superimposed on this world. Nor is it
a process of "spiritual" or "internal" change that will
leave the outer realities looking much the same. It
is the liberation of the world we live in, know, touch,
smell, suffer, from all that corrupts and destroys it.
— CHARLES ELLIOTT, *PRAYING THE KINGDOM*

A particular form of intercessory prayer, and one that can frequently flow most powerfully out of our own experience of pain, involves praying the news.

This means taking complete strangers — or whole groups of people or other situations from the national or international news — into your prayer.

Is it in any way meaningful to pray for situations that are completely beyond our control and have no direct bearing on our own life? Or have they? If it is true that we are "all one below the tide line," then whatever happens in other, troubled, parts of the world is part of our being-in-the-world. In the same way, our affairs, and the way we handle them, are part of what makes other people who they are. A blight on one branch of the tree has an effect on the tree as a whole and, therefore, on every other branch. A virus that affects our lungs will sooner or later lower the resistance and strength of every other part of the body.

And if it *is* meaningful to pray in such a way, how might we approach this kind of prayer? In this chapter we will look at two ways of praying the news. We will also reflect on the special power such prayer has when it flows from the heart of someone who has a real bond of empathy with the situation or person for which we are praying. Finally, we will look at ways of living out the dream toward which our prayer might beckon us, on behalf of those for whom we pray.

The Expanding Universe Method

This approach to praying the news begins in your own backyard and sees the local news in a larger context. Try reading your local newspaper or your parish magazine, or perhaps even something less official, such as the community bulletin board or newsletter.

Let's start with the local paper. Try noticing the issues that seem to be dominating peoples' thoughts and attention in your area. What, as the doctor might ask you, seems to be the trouble? Are there any natural or environmental problems in the news? Have your local politicians been making waves with recent decisions? Is there a particular crime that has roused a lot of emotion? Are any controversies brewing? What are they about?

In my town at present, for example, there are plans to build a bypass road that will make the journey to work much easier and faster for a few people. But it will also go straight past a school playground, putting children at risk from cars and their fumes. A common dilemma, but in this particular case there is an extra parameter that makes the whole issue into quite a cliff-hanger: A church owns a crucial few yards of land essential to the bypass, and the owners cannot be compelled to sell. The parishioners, and indeed many other local people, have made it clear to the parish priest that they do not approve the sale of this bit of land; the priest, having canvassed locally for opinions, has now put the peoples' case to the diocese. It remains to be seen how the diocese will decide.

Why should such a relatively minor matter cause you to hammer on heaven's door with prayers of intercession on behalf of either the bypass or the playground? This minor, local issue calls for discernment and decision making that form a small — *but accessible* — fragment of much larger, more far-reaching decisions. It demands that we face, here on our own doorstep, questions about what we really want, what we most value, and how we exercise what little power we have. We know that we can't single-handedly save the rain forests or prevent the oppression of minority peoples. But the people of that parish know that they *can* tell their parish priest what they think, and they can also make sure that their feelings get heard by those who will make the decision. A drop in the ocean, perhaps. But what is the ocean, if not a vast collection of drops?

Prayer about actual issues on our own doorstep can lead to action. Local action of this kind has a number of positive effects:

- It can achieve a change of heart in the real decision makers.

- It can make good things happen or prevent bad things from happening. Conversely, if this local power is not wielded with wisdom and love, it can do just the opposite, making bad things happen and preventing the good.

- It can empower ordinary people to exercise their own judgment and accept a degree of responsibility in matters that affect us all.

- It can harness the ideals and dreams of these same ordinary people on behalf of those who have no vote about how things are done: the children, the frail, the marginalized, and the inarticulate.

Such local action can become an effective sign of the coming of God's reign. How we respond on the local level matters not only because it has an impact locally, but also because local decisions have global consequences that we can almost never see or imagine at the time. We throw our pebble of involvement into the village stream, and it contributes to a tidal wave of reaction on beaches at the other end of the world. It *matters* how we throw our pebble!

And so a way to pray the news might be to reflect, over time, on a particular local issue that rouses your feelings and to let it grow until you see something of its global consequences. Notice, for example, what factors are influencing your own feelings and how these same factors reappear again and again, in different guises, in the big stories of international significance. Notice your own reactions, and then ask yourself: *Is my response likely to lead me and others to an increase or to a decrease of faith, hope, and love?* You can be sure that whatever increases the reign of love in your own home town will also increase it in the wider world, though you may never know through what invisible channels that power will flow.

And finally, when you find reactions in yourself that do seem to be leading closer to the reign of God, *act on them,* for all our sakes!

The Shrinking World Method

It is very easy to become overwhelmed by the international news and to be sucked into an abyss of despair when we become aware of our apparent helplessness to change things or even to alleviate the world's suffering in any significant way. A common and understandable reaction in these circumstances is to switch off inwardly—to insulate ourselves against an encroachment of grief and pain that we cannot bear. It follows, all too easily, that we become insensitive to some of the horrors we see on our television screens. We can grow dangerously apathetic and detached. If your reactions are anything like mine, you start to feel bad about yourself for not feeling more acutely what is happening to others in the world. Guilt kicks in and undermines any possibility of releasing positive energy into the troubled situation.

When I react like this, I find that it helps to take advantage of what the news editors call the human interest factor. In practice this means paying attention to the specific situation of a person or family caught up in the trouble. Every night there is a report from somewhere around the world of a natural disaster or a political crisis or a major atrocity or a ferocious crime. Before you shut off emotionally because of your own powerlessness, try to notice the face of someone caught in the middle of it. Notice the expression in his eyes. Imagine experiencing the cold sweat of her fear. See for yourself where this person is living. Notice the things he says. Enter into her domestic space for a while and let it become your prayer, just as you might pray for a friend.

When the hostility between Serbs and Croats in the former Yugoslavia was at its height, I remember feeling shamefully unmoved by much of what I was seeing and hearing in the daily news. Until one day I caught a snatch of conversation recorded by a reporter.

I was listening to the car radio. The horrifying statistics from Bosnia were passing through my brain but not really touching my heart. It was too much to cope with, and I knew I was screening it out. Then they interviewed a woman, who said how much easier it would be if they were fighting an "enemy" and not those who had seemed to be friends. She was fighting people with whom she had been drinking coffee only a few weeks ago.

Those words went straight to my gut. My feelings locked into the woman's, and I knew that I could pray for her in a real way. I could be with her over the coffee and in the shellfire, sharing something of her bitterness and despair. I could bring her pain to God, because she was too preoccupied to bring it herself. I understand about drinking coffee, and I understand about friends who turn sour on you. It wasn't much of a connection, but it was enough to connect us in prayer, and it was real.

So another way of praying the news, especially when the news is too much for you, might be to seek out a real person amid the carnage and let that one person's story, that one person's need, form your prayer of intercession. This will shrink the unmanageable down to a size that is unavoidable. It will hurt, but maybe real prayer such as this has to hurt, just as Christ's prayer for us from the cross was a hurting prayer.

When unemployment shook our personal securities a few years ago, I remember being deeply moved by a small, handmade card from a friend. It read:

I am only one,
but I am one.
I cannot do everything,
but I can do something.
What I can do, I should do,
and with the help of God,
I will do.

That friend couldn't find a new job or pay our mortgage for us. He knew that, but he didn't let helplessness hold him away from us in our difficulty. And what he did do has been a living spring of encouragement and has made a real difference to our lives and our faith ever since. I don't suppose he ever imagined, when he included this profound little saying in the card, that these words would find their way into a book and that the loaves and fishes he gave to us when we were hungry would possibly feed hundreds of unknown strangers.

Even the small gesture, expressed from the reaches of our hearts, can do more than we hope for or imagine, when it is made in the power of God.

Living Water from a Hard Rock

Reports of devastation and disaster in the world can prompt guilt. Others are starving, and we feel guilty about enjoying our dinner. Guilt because we are living comfortably, while others struggle in the wake of a typhoon or quake as their homes are plundered by a murdering army. Whole nations face financial ruin, while we worry about the moral dilemma of having savings or investments. Such guilt is common but never productive. But there are other ways of being alongside these overwhelming troubles in the world that *are* productive and deeply meaningful. I encountered such a way one day during a retreat.

On the face of it, my situation was a million miles removed from the devastating events going on at the time in the "real world," and in Bosnia particularly, which was under heavy bombardment. We were a group of people who had deliberately gone into seclusion for eight days of silent prayer. We broke the solitude and silence only once daily to come together for the Eucharist, during which we were invited to offer our own petitions and intercessions. A hollow gesture?

One day, among the usual prayers for friends who were sick or in need, a new and faltering voice broke through. "Lord, we remember the people of Bosnia . . . we pray for the children especially . . . the babies and toddlers under bombardment, we bring you their terror, their panic. Lord, hear us . . ." and the voice trailed off into brokenness. For a few moments, a total silence descended on the chapel. Each one of us was caught up in that heartrending cry to heaven. The power of that prayer electrified all who heard it. The man who prayed was present with those he prayed for in a way that we couldn't begin to understand but that we recognized immediately.

There was a simple, yet sacred, explanation for the power of this man's prayer. As a toddler in 1944, he had been in an isolation hospital with scarlet fever when the hospital was bombed. In his prayer he was expressing the kind of empathy that can grow only from experience. His own childhood terrors were being lived out again in his prayer for the Bosnian babies, but it had been transformed into a Calvary prayer that could have come straight from the heart of the Lord: "Father I *know* where they are. I *am* where they are. I bring them to you."

Living Out the Dream

During the early 1990s, a British army officer serving with the United Nations peacekeeping forces in Bosnia was fired by the desire to rebuild an orphanage. It had been destroyed by shellfire, and the surviving children had been evacuated far from their home town. The story was retold in a television program titled "Against the Odds."

The program reenacted scenes from the drama, beginning with the soldier's enthusiastic, and perhaps rash, promise to thirty children that he would give them back their home. Thirty hurting children, who had lost everything in the war and seen their parents slaughtered and their homes destroyed. Their faces lit up in a mixture of hope and disbelief when they heard the soldier's promise. They watched and joined in as the men in the officer's command cleared the ruined building and readied it for reconstruction. And the soldiers became deeply attached to the children, played football with them, talked to them, and began to love them.

The children knew nothing of the terrible struggles being played out behind the scenes to raise the £250,000 needed to fund the project. Nothing of the negotiations with the Bosnian government, the British government, the European Community. Nothing of the countless fund-raising ventures started on their behalf. They had no idea of the cost of their housing, and if they had known, such a figure would have been beyond their comprehension.

The site was cleared, but no building was begun. The soldiers were posted elsewhere. They were forced to leave the children behind, with just their promise, still unfulfilled, and their love. The tough faces of the fighting troops were streaked with tears that day.

The officer whose dream it had been gave up his commission, his job, his family life, and his reputation. He stayed behind on the site — because he had promised.

There was hope. There was funding. There was progress. And then the blow fell. The architect announced that the cost would be four times what had been estimated. A million pounds would be needed to complete the project. And the reason was simple: The orphanage, before its destruction, had been a protected historic building. If it was to be restored at all, it must be restored perfectly. It must become once again the perfect thing its first architect had dreamed it to be. And the cost of perfection was astronomical.

The European Union backed off. The Bosnian government stalled. But the bazaars and the rummage sales went on. The project went ahead on blind faith with barely sufficient funds to pay for the initial stages. And month by month the pennies in the collection boxes shamed larger sums out of the institutional pockets. The price was paid in full, the home was restored in its perfection, and the broken ones came back to their roots and rediscovered the lost heart of their hoping.

It was a modern parable. A story of destruction redeemed and restored. An exodus in loneliness and terror and a return of the lost ones to the promised land. A challenge to reach for perfection and a cost that stretches us beyond our limits. Above all, it was a parable of covenant love — the love that delivers what it has promised, however high the cost, however impossible the odds.

It leads me to believe that when we pray the news our smallness can *count,* and, like the widow's mite and the rummage sales, become the drop that causes the ocean to overflow. It plants in my heart the truth that when we live out the dream in our own lives, we are living God's dream for creation. When this is our focus, then two column inches in a newspaper can become the space that saves.

❧ TAKING IT FURTHER ❧

Take it into prayer

Try browsing through your local newspaper or tuning in to your local radio station. Does anything you read or hear attract your attention?

If so, try taking it into prayer, but not simply in a straightforward request to God to sort it out. Instead, let yourself spend ten minutes or so in silent, relaxed meditation, imagining yourself to be a participant in the issue you have been reading or hearing about. Where do you find yourself? What, if anything, do you feel like saying to the other people involved? Listen to anything you think they might be wanting to say to you.

Take a balloon ride

Now let yourself float up in a hot air balloon. Look down on your own town or village and take a more distanced view of what is going on down there. Gradually, as you float higher, imagine more and more of the world coming into view. How does what is happening in your own small community affect the world around it? Do you notice any connections?

Finally, let the balloon take you to God the Father, looking down on the world he has created, seeing all the connections and all the effects of what is happening everywhere. In your prayer now, ask God to place you with his Son. Let Jesus step into the balloon basket with you, and then gradually float back down to the earth, back to your own town, back to your own fireside and the newspaper or radio beside you. You are back where you started, but you are not alone anymore. How do you feel about things now? Is there any way in which you and Jesus together might make a difference?

Notice one item

If you watch the television news in the evening, make a habit of noticing one item of news that draws you more than the others. Out of all that you are seeing on the screen, notice one particular face or one person's story. Let yourself be drawn into that story. Try walking in the other person's shoes for a mile or two. Hold her face in your memory. Later, as you carry this incident or situation to God, focus on that single face and that personal story, as if it were happening to your closest friend.

In this way you will, in the mystery of things, be walking alongside that person in a way that brings both of you into the unseen presence of God. In the film *Schindler's List,* the comment is made that "To have saved a single soul is to have saved the world entire." When you carry in your heart one person caught up in tragedy, you carry in your heart the whole tragic situation.

The person you are carrying is becoming a part of you. Can you do anything, however small, to ease her pain and the pain of her people?

ADDITIONAL READING

Praying the Kingdom, by Charles Elliott (London: Darton, Longman, & Todd, 1985).

Making a Habit of Instant Prayer

A quiver full of arrows

---

*

> He who binds to himself a joy
> Doth the winged life destroy.
> He who kisses a joy as it flies
> Lives in eternity's sunrise.
>
> — WILLIAM BLAKE

A few things stick in our memories forever. I'll never forget one lesson about prayer in Confirmation class when I was an adolescent. Only one thing really took root in me at that time, and that was the encouragement to make short, quick "arrow prayers." Perhaps it was the only method I felt I had a chance of turning into reality. And so, ever since then, I have shot my arrows Godward at times of special need or concern. Perhaps like many other people, I instinctively shoot off such arrows every time I hear an ambulance siren. Does such emergency prayer have any meaning? Is it *real*?

Fingertip Prayer

Since the so-called Velvet Revolution of 1989, which freed Czechoslovakia from the grip of totalitarianism, in Prague's Wenceslas Square a little shrine to the victims of the uprising is marked by a powerful sculpture showing hands reaching up to the heavens out of some unseen, unfathomed pit.

This sculpture reminds me of times when I have reached up to God like that, out of my despair or shame or need, with just my fingertips reaching above the all-engulfing troubles and confusions. But it was enough. It was all God needed to draw me to himself. Reaching out for freedom from the hopelessness of totalitarianism — it was all they needed too, the martyrs of Prague. For them as for me, the sculpture represents a desire rooted deep in the heart — a desire for freedom, a desire for peace.

Desire *is* prayer, fingertip prayer — small signals of need invoking God's presence in our days, small signals of need expressing our desire to become *aware* of God's constant presence. Surely such emergency calls reach God's ears! But not because God needs to be reminded of his duties, as though God were some remote and dispassionate official. Not because God needs *me* to let him know that someone is, even this minute, being rushed to the hospital through the streets of my home town.

A familiar scene from family life may come nearer to the truth about what is really happening when we stretch out our fingertips to God in this way. Small children can try our patience to its limits in their stubborn determination to have their own way. Teenagers can do even better, in their adamant refusal to discover the world by any route except their own. Parents of children in both these age groups deserve special commendation. Imagine then, this scene . . .

A family outing perhaps, planned around a picnic in the park. After the first hour or so, boredom sets in. The six-year-old wants to join in a boisterous game with his elder siblings and gets hurt in the process. There are tears and bruises. A ten-year-old starts to whine about missing her favorite TV program and wants to know how long they have to stay in this silly park. And the fourteen-year-old takes off without a word and goes missing for a couple of hours. By midafternoon the family returns, thoroughly depressed, to the pile of breakfast dishes and the prospect of a sullen evening ahead.

But, come bedtime, something changes. The six-year-old unexpectedly flings his arms round his mother's neck as she tucks him into bed. Nothing is said, but she knows that something has been restored. The ten-year-old slips into the kitchen and does the washing up. Nothing is said, but the signal is understood. The fourteen-year-old summons all his courage and humility together and asks his father's help with a difficult situation at school that has been troubling him all day. And the parents? Well, maybe they were only waiting to be asked, because until that moment of breakthrough they knew that the children would resist everything they might give.

Fingertip prayer can signal just such a moment of breakthrough, a way of telling God, and ourselves, that our resistance has been breached; we acknowledge our need and our desire to talk with him, our desire for a restored relationship. Every mother knows the formidable strength of a baby's tiny finger — sufficient power to harness her full-time, undivided attention and to capture her unconditional love. So it is with God.

From time to time, I have sat through auction sales, and there too I have seen the delicate sensitivity of the almost wordless interaction between auctioneer and bidder. The language is so muted, barely visible, but the auctioneer's eye is trained and watchful for the slightest indication of intention to buy; the auctioneer is alert to the merest possibility of interest. When I think of the dynamics of the auction room, it reassures me that God too will react to my faltering fingertips. He knows when I turn my attention toward him, even when I hardly know it myself. My fingertip prayer speaks to him more clearly than if I were to stand up in the salesroom and make a huge scene.

I have seen bidders buy mansions with their fingers. I have seen them commit hundreds of thousands of pounds with the slightest inclination of their heads. And I know now, albeit with hindsight, that my silent, slight movements of longing, need, and joy have always reached the God who first nudged them in me. And I know that God's response is out of all proportion to my bid.

Fingertip prayer has sometimes lifted me out of that dark abyss as surely as the flame of resistance lifted the Prague martyrs out of totalitarian control. And fingertip prayer has also committed me to pay the price of my desires. For we may reach out our fingers in our own need, but when God has responded by drawing us to himself, we become extensions of God's eyes and hands, commissioned to notice the fleeting, wavering movements of others' fingers and to help him draw them safely home.

Be warned, therefore. When you raise your finger in the auction room of prayer, you may be committing yourself to pay the market price for your desire. Perhaps it is even true to say that God always answers our fingertip prayers, but we are not always willing to pay the price of those answers. We want the results, but the checkbook remains firmly hidden in our back pockets. No one ever promised us that prayer would come cheap!

And when you fling your arrows at God, they may return to you like boomerangs, pointing out, not always gently, that the help you beg for someone else may be forthcoming only through *your* action and intervention.

I remember especially one arrow prayer that I once shot off to God on behalf of someone who was desperately seeking help and guidance and encouragement. I dispatched an urgent request to God. Soon afterwards I was meditating on the miracle of the feeding of the five thousand (Luke 9:10 – 17). If you remember, the disciples tell Jesus that the crowd is hungry and ask him to do something about the situation. He replies: "Feed them yourselves." These words entered my heart like my own arrow returning to me as a boomerang, carrying God's response.

Kingfisher Moments

Not all instant prayer is about our emergencies. A friend once described moments of sudden awareness of God's power and presence as kingfisher moments — like darts of brilliance streaking across the riverbank, caught for a split second in the full light of the sun. These moments can be occasions for spontaneous prayer. These prayers are not of urgent petition but of sudden praise.

Following are a couple of my kingfisher moments. Do they strike a chord in you? Do any of your own come to mind?

> What a morning it was! A rare and joy-filled morning for a win-ter-wearied world. I felt resentful that I had to spend it at a desk, buried in a tower of air-conditioned offices. Yet if I hadn't had to drive in to Manchester that morning, I would have missed the roadside banquet of blossom, birdsong, and the overflowing exu-berance of spring.

It ought to have been a day for lingering and sauntering, sniffing and savoring, but inevitably I myself was rushed and I rushed along with the traffic. And perhaps it was good, because it was precisely because of the speed that I noticed the horse. It was just a split-second flash of awareness as I sped by, but it left me thrilling with the moment's glory. He was standing near the edge of the field, his head raised high, proud yet unself-conscious, above the hedgerow. And the rising sunlight was right behind him, setting him into stark relief against the greens and whites and pinks of grass and blossom.

I passed. And as I passed, the sun lit up his head and I saw every bristle on his chin alive with silver, as if transfigured by the touch of eternity. I gasped at the suddenness of the vision and Jesus' promise drifted through my mind: "Every hair on your head has been counted" (Luke 12:7). Not only counted, but cherished and valued as if every hair were the *only* hair, and every horse the perfect horse.

It was a resurrection moment, and it brought my whole day to life. In all the cart-horse lumbering, blundering days that would follow, I have often returned to this perfect moment of the silver bristles and remembered what I knew in that instant: that such times are moments of reality that run through all the mud and the mess and the muddle like a seam of gold.

The light was red at the first intersection. I had to wait for a few minutes — it seemed like minutes but I suppose it was only seconds — at the head of the line of cars, opposite the house that had always intrigued me. It must have been a day-care center, because I would often see small children being dropped off there at this time in the morning; in the summer afternoons there was usually a crop of youngsters playing in the steeply rising back garden.

I watched the place again that morning, not having much else to occupy my mind until the light turned green. There were no children in sight, but a little cat sat in solitary splendor on an upstairs windowsill. For a moment I held her gaze, or she held mine! Then she was gone, back to her haunts in the unseen spaces of the unknown house. I had seen her before, very occasionally, when she happened to be sitting on the windowsill at the same moment I happened to be sitting in the traffic line.

But that morning she reminded me of God. Prayer seems like that. There are moments when we see God and know his reality in a new kind of way. God shows himself to us when we least expect it. He sits for a moment on the windowsill. And we receive the fleeting gift because we are also sitting still — usually because of some immobilizing circumstance and the much-resented red lights that turn out to be graced moments after all.

I recall thinking that I had to remember to tell my daughter about the cat that night. But why should she believe me? She would need to see it for herself. If she had seen it, even once, she would *know* that it was truly there, however invisible most of the time. And we, too, do need the glimpses that God gives us of himself. They are enough to assure us of his permanent reality, however infrequent our sightings may be.

The light turned green. The moment of eternity was passed, and I was back in time again, but I was carrying a new knowledge in my heart, not only of the occupants of this one house, but also of the ways of God.

On another occasion, I was on my way to visit a friend on a drab estate on the outskirts of a drab town. It was trash pickup day, and all the dumpsters were lined up on the street. It was just a day or two before Christmas — a rare, crisp, cold, clear morning. As I drove slowly along the road, looking for my friend's house, I was suddenly stopped (literally) in my tracks by the overwhelming vision of a huge cobweb, draped over one of the dumpsters and transfigured by the frost and the sunlight. A kingfisher moment that gladdened my heart that morning as if in anticipation of the bells on Christmas Eve.

There was never any danger of my forgetting such a moment of glory, but I was reminded of it again several years later in a group of people who were tentatively beginning to share their experience of prayer with each other. One of them was silent for a long time. When she gathered the courage to say something about how she felt she had encountered God during the week, she told us, shyly, how she had been driving to work one cold morning, beneath a gray December sky. Gradually her windshield had iced up, and she had been forced to stop and defrost it. As she bent to get the scraper, she noticed a small patch of blue sky, allowing a streak of sunlight to fall to the earth below. And then she noticed on her windshield the perfect filigree pattern of the frost crystals, which left her momentarily breathless at their intricacy.

The commonplace is made holy, and moments of spontaneous joy come to us who behold it.

❧ TAKING IT FURTHER ❧

Stretch out your heart's fingers

In a few calm moments, perhaps in your daily review prayer, try to recall any times during the day when you prayed a spontaneous arrow prayer.

What were those arrows about? Need? Joy? Gratitude? Look closely at any needs you have shot at God today. Bring your need to God in the stillness of your evening prayer.

- If your arrow was on behalf of someone else, can you do anything to meet that person's needs?

- If your arrow was about your own need, can you now, in the stillness, recognize any ways that may be opening up to you to deal with the need you have expressed? Arrow prayers are shot off in the heat of the moment, but their answers may most frequently be discovered in the cool of reflection.

The value of arrow prayer may be that it has the power to pinpoint the center of *particular* needs, either in ourselves or in others. And once the center of the need is recognized, we are much more likely to be open to ways of dealing with it and much less resistant to God's action to heal and to nourish. Like the disciples, whom Jesus instructed to feed the crowds themselves, we may find that God is asking us to be the agents of miracles.

If you find sudden joys in your day, like my moment with the horse and with the cat at the traffic light, express your gratitude to God for this moment of revelation. These moments are life-giving in ways we cannot begin to understand, both for ourselves and for all creation. They are an overflow of God's own creative energy.

12

Going Deeper in Prayer

Zooming in

⁂

I have seen the sun break through
to illuminate a small field
for a while, and gone my way
and forgotten it. But that was the pearl of great price,
  the one field that had
the treasure in it. I realise now
that I must give all that I have
to possess it.

— R. S. Thomas, "The Bright Field"

Many people come to highly regard their experience in personal prayer. Something so important is worth more in-depth exploration. Here are a few ways that you might try to deepen your prayer.

Using the Metal Detector

We have already looked at the importance of taking time to reflect on what a period of prayer suggested to you about your relationship with God and how it connects to your daily experience. This reflective review can also help you find the best way to deepen your prayer.

If your review reveals any point or issue in the prayer experience that especially moved you positively or negatively, go back to that same point during your next time of prayer. This may be

God's call to you to explore a particular issue more fully. Make a mental note of any such points, so that you know where to return next time.

This process is a bit like using a metal detector. You have already established that there is treasure in a particular field (that is, in a particular experience of prayer). You want to dig for it, but you want to dig in the right spot in the field. Or you could compare it to using a Geiger counter to establish the location of high radioactivity.

To use such a "detector," just still yourself and then notice where exactly in the prayer you have (or had) a strong emotional reaction. Keep trying this and in time you will recognize intuitively the point in your prayer that felt the most significant. If the reaction seems to be strong but negative, don't abandon the exercise. A strong reaction is an important pointer for you, even if it feels painful. Trust God to be gentle in his dealings with you. He may dig into sensitive areas, but he will do so with tenderness.

The process of revisiting significant points in prayer is often called repetition; it may continue for many days. You may focus on a particular prayer experience or Gospel passage as you let your feelings draw you closer and closer to the heart of the matter. Don't try to repeat the whole prayer, as if to get a different slant on it; just stay with that one crucial moment or point that holds you, and ask God for the grace to see what meaning it carries for you.

Renewing Old Acquaintances

As I write, I have just enjoyed a day in a house where I often make retreats. Today I was there for only a few hours, mostly attending meetings. I had only a little free time, but then I did what I always do when I go back there: I walked along my favorite paths, noticing with renewed pleasure places where I have met God in prayer in particular ways and perhaps with special power.

Perhaps you have a similar place to which you like to return? It doesn't have to be a retreat house. Have you ever gone back to a place where you have spent happy times in the past — maybe a holiday resort that holds good memories for you or a childhood setting? As you seek out your special haunts, do the familiar places bring back the feelings you experienced during those times? Whether those feelings are painful or pleasant, they reinforce the memories, making them more firmly established and renewing your enthusiasm and energy for life here and now. For example, the experience of visiting your home town may stir vivid memories of friends you have lost touch with; those memories may provide the boost you need to get in touch with an old friend.

A very specific object, tune, or smell may bring back whole waves of memory. This is the metal-detector effect at work. The sudden discovery of an old toy, a forgotten letter, a snatch of a song, or the scent of hay or of a particular flower or perfume may evoke a strong response in your heart. If you could dig down at that very point in your heart's soil, you would surely find the source of the sudden flashback regarding a cherished relationship or a significant period.

In your life of prayer, return visits to the scenes and events of your prayer can be life-giving and life-renewing. Try noticing when and where your detector bleeps most insistently, and ask God to take you deeper.

Store up treasure for the future by making a point of noticing and treasuring times when you feel very close to God. These may be times when imaginative prayer leaps to life for you or when you feel that you are given sure guidance or new insight. Whatever gives rise to such experience, store it in your heart, because it will be an important resource for you in times to come.

Remember how we hear in the Gospel that Mary "treasured all these things and pondered them in her heart" (Luke 2:19)? Surely she drew on that store of graced memories when she stood at the foot of the cross. We do well to draw on her wisdom. When we are close to God, we are in spiritual consolation; we are standing in the sunlight of his presence. But the clouds will come down, inevitably — even though the sun is still there energizing us from behind the clouds. It is during the cloudy times that we so need the reassurance of our memories; we need to remember how it felt when we stood in the sunlight. So treasure your experiences of consolation and store them, like Mary, and ponder them in your heart. They will carry you through the Calvary times. They are part of God's loving provision for you.

The Diviner's Rod

The water diviner's rod is another metaphor of the process of repetition, or revisiting significant points in prayer. Repetition is like searching in the desert for the point where the rod registers the unseen presence of water. Of course the rod we use in the prayer of repetition is sensitive to the presence of the living water that Jesus urged us to seek. This divining rod must be held lightly, so every movement of our inner heart is registered and noticed. And the rod's tremor must be trusted and acted upon if the treasure is to be found.

Water divining, in this sense, is much the same as metal detecting. It can be done by following this simple process:

• Move slowly and sensitively across your prayer time.

• Stand still when you register a response.

• Dig further down at that point.

• Keep digging until you strike water.

How do you know when you have dug far enough? I suggest that, as in every other way of prayer, you will be able to judge your finding by its fruits. You will know when you are drawing on the living water because it will release life and energy in you. Receive this energy and let it renew your heart and turn your desire into reality. This is what it means to be a human being who is fully alive in spirit.

Digging for Rock

If you have ever observed someone building a house, you will know how much work goes into the foundation. It is essential to dig deep enough to find a solid surface. This is sometimes no problem, if there is firm ground or rock not too far below the surface. Sometimes the job can become a huge one, exacting great cost in money, energy, and time. There is no shortcut. If the foundation is unstable, the house will fall.

This experience also helps lead us into a better understanding of what repetition in prayer can mean. Sometimes my own prayer feels (if I look back over it honestly) as if I'm building an estate of unstable houses. Day by day I move on, with inordinate haste, from one shaky house to the next. When the next gale comes, the whole estate falls over like a pack of cards. I haven't taken the time or the trouble to be sure of the foundations on which I was so recklessly building.

How much more fruitful, for myself and for others, if I had stayed with just the one house and gone down deep enough to make it sure and stable. How much wiser if I had dug down to the rock before I constructed over it my own ideas and conclusions, like putting the roof on the house before there were walls to support it. How sad God must be, and how frustrated with me, when I lack the patience to simply wait and let him show me the foundations that should underpin my prayer.

It is sometimes easy and obvious to see the foundational truth that a particular prayer experience is showing you. Sometimes, however, it can take longer to get to the heart of the matter. You sense that there is more to discover. You feel the nudge to dig further down.

How do we know we've found stable ground in our prayer?

Let's suppose that you feel that your prayer has given you some new insight on dealing with a problematic relationship in your life. To test whether this insight is a sound foundation for action, try living it out and noticing your feelings and reactions. For example, whenever the difficult person crosses your path, recall that your prayer suggested a new way of dealing with him. Try out the new approach as far as you feel able to do so. See what happens. Does the reality of the live encounter confirm or negate the insight of your prayer?

Notice your feelings and reactions. Take them back into prayer and dig down, with God, further into the point where you are experiencing a strong reaction, either positive or negative. Take the matter further into prayer, each time homing in more specifically on the heart of the issue. As you do this, you are opening your heart to more insight and more precise guidance. Test it day by day. Will it stand the weight of experience? Is it making a real difference (however small)? Is it moving toward an increase of faith, hope, and love in you? Keep on digging in this way for as long as your prayer is yielding new growth on this issue.

Here are some questions to keep at the front of your mind as you dig like this in the prayer of repetition:

- What does this mean for me in practice?

- Where is the solid core of this prayer, on which I can build specific choices and decisions?

Not all prayer is about resolving issues. Frequently, repetition is more like sucking on a hard candy until you have extracted all its flavor. You know that you have come close to God; your inner Geiger counter will show you where this was happening most significantly. Then, in your prayer of repetition, the deeper truths and meanings of your prayer can be explored gradually.

❧ TAKING IT FURTHER ☙

The zoom lens

Imagine your prayer as a kind of zoom lens.

- Try focusing this lens on the memory of any moment or period when you felt a powerful sense of God's presence. Stay with the picture that your lens reveals. Reflect on this memory. Explore the details of what you see through your lens, as it magnifies this moment in your heart. Stay especially with any specific detail of the memory that attracts you and deepen that detail. Respond to God in whatever way feels right for you.

• Now bring back the focus to your current setting. Can you see how that graced moment has made a difference to your life? In what ways? How can you nourish the transformation that this moment began in you?

• Now focus your lens on a past period, a time when you felt trapped in potentially destructive circumstances or relationships. Notice in your prayer the feelings you had then: restlessness, anger, impatience, frustration, helplessness, despair. Without judging yourself or others, simply let these feelings be present to your memory and your prayer.

• Now refocus again on *today*. You have moved on from that past period, however you chose to handle it at the time. How has your life been since then? Did the destructive circumstances *actually* destroy you, or have you not only survived but grown since then? If you have survived and grown, how might this fact affect your reaction if you face destructive times again in the future? How might it affect your response to other people who are going through apparently destructive experiences?

PART THREE

Using the Word as Our Guide

In the previous part we looked at various ways of focusing our hearts in prayer. Some of these ways provided more understanding of ourselves and our experience, in the light of God's presence. Others helped us focus our prayer for others or for the events and needs of the world.

Another very powerful approach to prayer is to focus our hearts specifically on the Word of God as it is revealed to us, in his creation, in the Word of Scripture, or in conversation with him. Part 3 explores how to listen as God speaks God's Word to us, in various ways, in our own time and place.

13
Praying with Scripture

Pages of Life

※

*The study of the Bible might be transformed if we
could understand the biblical images not as poetical
ways of stating what could with greater precision
be stated in exact prose, but rather as powerful symbols
able to release a flow of spiritual life in us, if only
we will take them seriously and through imaginative
reflection open ourselves to their impact.*
— CHRISTOPHER BRYANT, *JUNG AND THE CHRISTIAN WAY*

There is a strange episode recounted by the prophet Ezekiel. He
is speaking of his own prayer and what he saw and heard as he
prayed one day. He heard a voice speaking and had a vision. The
voice said:

> "You, son of man, are to listen to what I say to you. . . .Open your
> mouth and eat what I am about to give you."
> When I looked, there was a hand stretching out to me, holding
> a scroll. He unrolled it in front of me. . . .
> He then said, "Son of man, eat what you see; eat this scroll,
> then go and speak to the House of Israel." I opened my mouth; he
> gave me the scroll to eat and then said, "Son of man, feed on this
> scroll which I am giving you and eat your fill." So I ate it, and it
> tasted sweet as honey.
> He then said, "Son of man, go to the House of Israel and tell
> them what I have said."
>
> (Ezekiel 2:8 – 3:4)

We could disregard this description as merely Ezekiel's personal flight of imagination, full of rather bizarre imagery at that. But if we do, we may miss something that is important and universal, especially about how we might pray with Scripture.

Let's look at the way Ezekiel engages with his vision. First he hears the voice of God; then he responds by listening. Then he sees the hand that holds the scroll, and he responds by receiving what is being offered. Next he tastes what has been placed in his mouth, and he responds by delighting in its sweetness. And finally he is commissioned to turn what he has experienced into food for the whole people of Israel. These observations highlight at least three ways of being open to God in our prayer:

- We are invited to use our *senses*. Ezekiel receives the revelation from God through his senses of sight, hearing, and taste. Opening our five senses to God can bring new dimensions to our prayer.

- We are invited to *respond* to what we are receiving. This is a two-way interaction. Prayer is not simply downloaded to us like information from the Internet. It is the gateway to an interactive relationship; we can turn prayer into a conversation.

- We are commissioned to turn our prayer into *action*. Like Ezekiel, we are asked to realize that prayer is not given primarily for ourselves and our personal spiritual growth, but for all God's world, and, very specifically, for that bit of God's world in which we "live, and move, and have our being" (Acts 17:28 KJV). For Ezekiel this was Israel. Where is it for us?

In the Beginning Is the Word

Ezekiel's prayer vision can take us, if we let it, back to our beginnings and beyond. "In the beginning was the Word: and the Word was with God and the Word was God" (John 1:1). And it can point toward many different ways of praying with that same Word.

That first Word (who is also the final Word, the Alpha and Omega — first and last — of all that is) was spoken in creation, expressing himself in every rock and flower, every star and slug that was to transform the emptiness of space into a living, teeming universe. And so we discover God, the speaker of the Word, in the many faces of God's creation.

Then the Word was spoken in the words of our own languages in the writings of Scripture and through the mouths of the prophets. God's covenant relationship with God's people was unfolded, conversation by conversation, through those who were willing to listen to him in prayer and respond to what they heard.

And when the time was right, the Word became incarnate in Jesus — God's own self, living among us, dying at our hands, and pouring out his Spirit through all the ages still to come. Jesus gives himself as a living sacrifice, which we continue to receive in the Eucharist, when, like Ezekiel, we "take and eat" the living Word, letting him become wholly incorporated into who we are.

Finally, having acknowledged our desire to be at one with the Word in a personal way, in prayer and in the Sacrament, *we* become words of the Word. We are called to let our lives become expressions of the Word, to speak the Word in what we say and do, and to share it, a living communion, with those who are hungry.

How do we translate these high ideals into real prayer?

In later chapters we will look at some possibilities in more detail, but in summary we might notice several ways in which we can encounter the Word and let that encounter become prayer:

- We can engage with God through his self-expression in creation. We can find God in all things.

- We can savor the Word as it is given to us in Scripture, by, as it were, tasting it, letting it dissolve in our hearts, and fill us with its meaning for us, just as Ezekiel savored the scroll.

- We can enter into a living encounter with the Jesus of the Gospels, by becoming, in our imagination, participants in the Gospel scenes.

- We can engage in personal conversation with God in prayer, letting God's Word invite our response, talking through with him the things that concern us.

- We can encounter the Lord in the Word of Calvary, hearing in our own lives and in the world's agony the echo of the dreadful "My God, my God, why have you forsaken me?" (Matthew 27:46).

- We can explore the ways in which we are being asked to turn our contemplation into action, for the sake of all God's people.

- We can come to the point where our words fade into the silence of simply being in the presence of God.

The Word around Us

Sometimes, when I wake up in the morning or take a walk in the woods or notice the expressions of the people I meet in the market, I think that God has written his signature in every corner of creation. Sometimes this signature is obvious, as, for example, in a summer dawn or a silent moonlit night or the grasp of a new-born baby's fingers. Sometimes we have to search for it among the debris of our dreams. Sometimes God's self-expression in the eyes of his children has been overlaid by the grief, need, and pain we have inflicted on each other, and only unconditional love can dissolve that layer of resistance that obscures God's face.

Whether easy or arduous, the search is worth the trouble! Those who know Saint Paul's Cathedral in London will be familiar with the famous epitaph to its architect, Sir Christopher Wren: "If you are looking for his memorial, look around you." The same can be said for God, with the one important difference that what we discover of God when we look around us is not his memorial but the traces of his living presence that is continually creating all that is.

There are clues to the kingdom everywhere around us, waiting to be discovered in each day. Some ways of searching out those clues are explored in chapter 14.

Savoring the Word

When I read about Ezekiel's vision, I can almost sense him rolling the scroll around in his mouth and discovering the power of its flavor — surprised, no doubt, that this dry piece of paper should yield such sweetness.

We too, when we hold a Bible in our hands and flick through its thin pages, might be forgiven for wondering how these dry scrolls are ever going to taste sweet! As for taking them into ourselves — reading, marking, and *inwardly digesting* them, as we're admonished to do in the *Book of Common Prayer* — that doesn't sound like an appealing enterprise at all.

Well, there is some good news on this front. There are ways of doing just that, of taking a few words from these dry pages, savoring them in our hearts until we have extracted their secrets, and then letting those secrets open up the ways we live and relate to each other. You might like to look at the suggestions in chapter 15.

Living with the Word

It would have been so different, of course, if we had actually walked with Jesus, heard him speak, and been present when he healed the sick and raised the dead and called the brokenhearted back into the fullness of life. If we could have eaten and drunk with him, sat in the boat with him, seen him laugh and cry, and witnessed his toughness and tenderness, then it would be so much easier to follow him with conviction.

Is it really so impossible? We can't turn the clock back. But we are seeking relationship in prayer with the Word who *is,* not with someone who merely *was* or with some perfect state that remains veiled in the future. We journey with the One who is with us in the present moment, and one way of praying with Scripture is to enter the Gospel scenes (or other places) in our imagination and let ourselves in prayer become participants in that scene. It is a way of being present to those events and letting them affect us as they might have affected us if we had been present when they first happened. And it is a most powerful way of entering into an intimate relationship with the Jesus of the Gospels. It can both surprise and transform us.

An approach to this form of scriptural prayer is suggested in chapter 16.

Word and Response

Ezekiel may well have been amazed into silence by the encounter with the scroll, but in other places he, and many other prophets and Old Testament figures, had no hesitation in talking with God — and in giving him the benefit of their opinions, if need be, on how things should be arranged! I guess most of us do the same, from time to time, especially when God seems to need a hand in getting things right.

So what are our own conversations like? When I look at some of my prayer conversations, I see something that looks more like monologue than dialogue and that tends not to let the Word get in edgewise. If I do let God have his say at all, and if I have the grace to listen while he speaks, how do I know that it is really God who is speaking in my heart and not just a kind of play that I have scripted myself?

When we enter prayer, we enter a relationship with God, and relationship leads to dialogue. Some ways of making this dialogue truly two-way and for testing its reality and validity are suggested in chapter 17.

The Word from the Cross

The most agonizing word of God was spoken on Calvary and continues to be uttered in the pain of his children, being lived out in every corner of his creation through all time. Prayer is hard when life hurts. And when we are least able to pray, we need prayer the most.

In chapter 18 we look at some ways of finding that much-needed prayer when our lives seem broken beyond repair.

Word into Action

God didn't stop at making himself known through his creation or through the words of his prophets. When our fallenness had alienated us from his presence, he took our human form and, as it were, rolled up his sleeves and got to work on the mess we had made of ourselves, our world, and each other. He became the child who taught the temple elders, the man with the callused hands and carpenter's apron, and the one who mysteriously breathed his very breath into us and commissioned us to do for each other what he has done for us himself.

If we take this commissioning seriously, we must acknowledge—in awe and humility—that *we* are being asked to become a channel for making the eternal Word incarnate in our own town and generation. We are asked to speak the Word to others in their own language and local dialect. And we are being asked to turn the words of our prayer into action for our world, just as the first Word did when he lived among us in human form. A tall order, but when we walk with God, we walk tall enough to see the vision beyond the horizon.

This is contemplation in action, and it is explored more fully in chapter 19.

Word into Silence

The more we learn to listen, the more we will realize that what God has to say in our hearts is far more worth listening to than our own barrage of requests and demands. And eventually we will pass from the desire to listen into the desire merely to *be* in God's presence. An approach to this kind of contemplation is explored in chapter 20.

The river deepens and widens and eventually streams back into the ocean, which is both its source and destination. Prayer moves into contemplation. Contemplation opens into transformation. We have tried to respond to the invitation made to us, as to Ezekiel, to take the Word into ourselves. And in response, that same Word takes us into himself for all eternity.

❧ TAKING IT FURTHER ❧

Notice your reactions

Notice your initial emotional reactions to some of the possibilities mentioned in this chapter: that you might enter into a two-way conversation with God on a regular basis; that you might enter the Gospel scenes as if you were really there; that you are being called to become part of the way in which God's Word is becoming incarnate, even now, in his world.

Simply notice — maybe write down — how you are reacting. Don't make any judgment about your reactions, and don't try to sanitize your feelings by tweaking them into what you think is the right reaction. Later, when you have had a chance to delve further into some of these forms of prayer, come back to these initial reactions and compare them with how you feel then.

Carry Scripture with you

Do you have a favorite passage of Scripture? If so, look it up and write it on a slip of paper you can keep with you. The Jews of Jesus' time used to keep Scripture texts in little boxes strapped to their foreheads so that they could always carry the Word with them in a tangible way. Try carrying your favorite part of the Word with you in some way. Every so often take it out, read it slowly, savoring its words and syllables and its meaning for you. Taste its sweetness and let it become a part of who you are.

14

Finding God in All Things

Clues to the kingdom

※

It takes practice to spot angelic presences. But practice alone is not enough, unless one can practice being taken by surprise.

— ALAN JONES, SOUL MAKING

Jesus told us that to have seen him was to have seen the Father (John 14:9). In his personality and ministry and in the stories he told, he showed us again and again something of what God and God's kingdom are like. And I would suggest to you that everything—every creature, person, and situation—has the power to reveal something, however small, of what God is like, if, as Jesus said, we have eyes to see and ears to hear.

Saint Paul says the same thing: "Ever since the creation of the world, the invisible existence of God and his everlasting power have been clearly seen by the mind's understanding of created things" (Romans 1:20). If this is true, it offers us a thrilling challenge.

Something you experience during the coming week will be an important clue for you as you search for signs of God. Something will cross your path or catch your attention that will show you something of the nature and mystery of God. It may be just a tiny piece in a vast jigsaw, but without it the puzzle cannot be completed. It is up to you to find it and claim it and then to share it with your fellow seekers. Try looking out for that one special moment or incident or feeling that is labeled: *This is what God is*

111

like. You could call them *parable moments,* and if you were asked to teach other people about God, you could use these parables to show them, in familiar pictures, how you have met God and known him.

With our mortal eyes, we will never see the full picture. That doesn't mean we shouldn't notice the pieces that come our way. Keep your eyes open and you can find something of God in *all* things and in all situations.

Look out for things that say something to you about: what God is like; what God's kingdom is like; what God is asking you to be.

The following sections give examples of places you might look for evidence of God and his kingdom.

In the Pavement Cracks

For some time after my father's death, my mother was quite depressed and turned in on herself. It was a struggle to encourage her to move beyond her understandable preoccupation with her negative feelings. Then one day she phoned me out of the blue, and she told me that she had been shopping that morning and had noticed a tiny, pink wild rose flowering shyly between two pavement stones.

At the time I was overjoyed to hear her obvious delight in noticing this little sign of grace, although neither she nor I would have consciously registered this as a moment of prayer. Yet it was. I can see that clearly now, and I'm glad to say that she too came to recognize the moment for the gift that it was.

Why was it prayer, rather than just a satisfying moment of observation? Well, I think three aspects of this encounter suggest that it was a moment given by God:

- The moment with the rose *made a difference* — to Mother and to me. It had something to say that we needed to hear. It said that the beauty and resilience and determination of life will assert themselves against the hardest resistance and obstruction and will find a way to grow and bloom.

- The meeting with the rose came at just the moment when Mother was ready to receive it, and it worked on her in complete harmony with the general pattern of the healing process that was taking place in her. It was *consistent* with all that God was already doing for her and in her.

- Recognizing the rose and its tenacious, exuberant hold on life left Mother feeling more at peace with herself and with the created world around her. And this was *an effect that didn't fade away but grew stronger* as the weeks and months and even years passed. She would remind me of the incident long afterwards and tell me how it had helped change the course of her desolation.

And so the rose became a kind of icon for my mother. Whenever she saw a wild rose after that, she remembered that life is truly stronger than death and that gentle perseverance is more powerful than strong resistance. We could say, with truth, that in the little rose she had glimpsed something of what God is like and of the values that reign in God's kingdom.

In the Workplace

I have a colleague whose hobby is woodworking. He can go to the lumberyard and pick up a grimy, weather-beaten lump of timber, hold it in his hands, look at it closely, and then see what it can be turned into on his lathe.

He tells me that, as he works the wood, he has to let it speak for itself, so that the transforming work becomes a kind of silent conversation between the wood and the woodworker. Bit by bit, the wood reveals its innermost pattern and texture. As it does so, the woodturner is continually reflecting on what shape is evolving out of its shapelessness and how best to bring out the wood's hidden beauty. If he is wise, he will let the wood cooperate. The two are partners in the creative act.

My colleague isn't a believer, but when I hear him talk about his hobby and see the joy in his eyes as he tells me about his latest project, I know that I am seeing a picture of how God deals with us — how he holds the weather-scarred, unformed lumps of us in his hands and sees the true reality at the heart of us. And he calls us into a relationship of ongoing cooperation with him as this transformation, this re-creation, is gradually brought about.

In listening to my colleague's thrilled awareness of the potential he holds in his hands, I see God's joy in what he sees hidden in the depths of each of us.

In the Marketplace

A friend of mine was eager to tell me that she had found a picture hanging in a shop that had appealed to her so much that she knew she had to buy it and take it home. It was a picture of Jesus sitting at a well with two little children beside him. She had a vague memory of having seen the picture before somewhere when she was a child herself. That drew her, but even more, she was drawn by the uncomplicated, unconditional love that the artist had brushed into the faces of the three figures at the well.

The merchant wanted sixteen pounds for the picture. My friend didn't have that much. And anyway, as her husband pointed out, the picture was very dirty and in urgent need of a new frame. In fact, you couldn't see the details or the beauty of the thing at all, because it was overlaid with grime and dust. They offered nine pounds for it, and their offer was accepted. My friend walked off clutching the picture.

Once home, they cleaned the picture and revarnished the frame, then hung it on their wall. They would never point out the picture when visitors came, but again and again people — not necessarily believers — would stand and gaze at the picture as if they were seeing something dearly loved but long lost and forgotten. There was no need to say anything. My friend simply let the picture speak for itself and allowed her guests to listen to its meanings for them.

My friend knew that the story of this picture was also a story about God and us, about how much he desires us, even when we are unrecognizable beneath the layer of sin and shame that disfigures us. How he comes to the market and will not go home until he has redeemed us. How gently he cleanses and restores us and places us in the heart of his Father's house. And how he rejoices when other people stop and gaze and recognize something of our creator's image in us.

On the Television

Alison Hargreaves, a young climber, lost her life on K2, one of the high Himalayan peaks, after reaching the summit. Some months later her widower and two small children went back to visit the mountain where their mother's body — never found — would always remain. This visit was filmed and screened on television.

There was a particularly moving moment when the family made a little stone memorial, where they intended to leave their last tributes and gifts to her. When it was ready, her daughter, Kate, aged four, spoke up and said that, because sweets were her own favorite thing and she wanted to give her favorite thing to her mummy, she was going to leave behind a candy.

As she laid her sweet beneath the stones, I was reminded of our need to express love and our desire to give to God, and to those we love, what we value most. At first, the scene seems almost ludicrous. Our sweets on God's mountain? I pondered these thoughts as I watched the sunrise light up the magnificent profile of K2, where Kate's sacrificial sweet lay. What can our tiny gestures of love possibly mean to God, our Father and the Lord of all creation?

Then my mother-heart felt an unmistakable contraction. I remembered how it feels when your child comes to you, mutely or inarticulately, clutching her most treasured prize, and places it in your hands with upturned gaze and eyes full of pride and joy and a trusting expectation that you will accept and welcome the gift.

Then I knew, not only how Alison Hargreaves felt when her Kate left a candy for her in the snow, but how God feels when we bring him our tiny offerings of love and lay them on the broad breast of his love for us. From a television program about a family of strangers, I had learned what it means to love and to praise the God of love, and also why Jesus urges us to become as little children.

And in Our Accidents

I can still remember the day I broke my driving glasses. One minute they were safely in my hands. The next, they were in pieces on the back stoop.

That was the end of my carefully arranged plans for the day. I couldn't drive, which meant I couldn't go to work or do any of the things I had planned to do. I was brought face to face with my complete dependence on something as simple as a pair of glasses. I suppose I had thought of myself as an independent working woman, well able to earn my living and look after my family and myself. Those illusions were shattered that morning, along with the glass on the stoop.

The hassle that ensued to get the problem solved gave me some time to think about my utter dependence on people and on gifts that are not mine to claim. I was able to do something about the problem but only because:

- There was an optician in town who had the skill and knowledge to prescribe new glasses for me.

- There were people who could make them and were willing to exert all their efforts over the next few days to make them quickly for me, a stranger who had been clumsy and careless.

- I could afford to pay for these services.

It sobered me to think that I am one of a small minority of people for whom these conditions apply. If I had lived in the Third World, or if I were unemployed or destitute in this country, I would just have had to live out my life in the hazy world in which my carelessness had stranded me.

This whole incident showed me something of my relationship with God and of my dependence on him. My outward sight, as well as my inward vision, is a pure gift from God, lent to me for a season and a purpose, and not mine at all. And we are gifts to each other, given for a purpose, to love and serve each other. Those few days of sightlessness blessed me with a different kind of insight. God spoke to me through my own carelessness and the implications of an everyday accident.

❧ TAKING IT FURTHER ❧

Where have you seen God?

God isn't playing hide-and-seek with us. He is there all the time. The problem is that our eyes are not always open to see him. When we look for him in our daily activities and situations, we become more aware of his presence.

- *Who has brought God's love to you this week?* We may experience his love, for example, in the neighbor who takes the trouble to ask how we are. Let us remember then that what is done for us by "the least" of God's creatures is done for us by God himself. His is the love that prompts their kindness to us and ours to them.

- *Which stories this week have shown you what God is like?* We may find God in the stories of people we know or see on television or read about in books or newspapers: stories of patience in the face of suffering, courage to stand up for justice, or hope and vision to make changes and inspire others to reach beyond themselves.

- *In what ways has God challenged you this week to change in some way?* We may hear God speaking to our hearts through our mistakes and accidents or even through our own wrongdoing. If we can tune ourselves to listen with humility, we will hear God's words of encouragement and forgiveness and learn from God how to respond, perhaps by changing attitudes toward ourselves or others.

- *What has God taught you about himself this week through one of his creatures?* Creation is a living description of the Creator. Trees show us how to thrust our roots down deep and not be satisfied with a shallow existence. The stars teach us that some things can be glimpsed only through the dark parts of our lives. Our family pet can help us see what it means to trust the one who loves us.

- *What has gone wrong for you this week, and has it shown you anything of God's ways of working in your life?* Often, like children in school, we learn most from our mistakes and the things we mess up. The things that go wrong sometimes have the effect of pulling away false certainty that makes us rely on ourselves rather than on God. In our apparent failures, we may see ourselves in a more truthful light; we may be less likely to be taken in by our own disguises. We may remember that the victory of our redemption was won in a place of shame and apparent total failure.

If you feel able to do so, choose a clue, or a jigsaw piece from your week's experience and share that special insight with a friend you trust, so that all God's people may be helped and encouraged to grow in their understanding of him and of his kingdom.

15

Discovering *Lectio Divina*

Out of the chocolate box

✴

A simple and time-honoured way of prayer which,
through a gentle unfolding, opens us to that deep level
of communication with the Divine.
— THELMA HALL, *TOO DEEP FOR WORDS —*
REDISCOVERING LECTIO DIVINA

As children, we were taught not to take the nicest cookies or the biggest strawberries, but the prayer I have called chocolate-box prayer invites us to do exactly that. God takes us to a well-spread table and says, "From all that you see, take what you most desire!"

Like the review prayer we have explored, and like the imaginative prayer that we will look at in chapter 16, chocolate-box prayer is a way of prayer that has been used traditionally for centuries and is known in textbook terms as *lectio divina* (divine reading). It traditionally involves praying with or meditating on a small portion of Scripture, perhaps just a few words or a single phrase that catches our attention in some way.

A Lesson from the Monks

Back in the times of the earliest monasteries, when almost no one was able to read, not even most monks, the brothers found an ingenious way of combining the daily Scripture reading with their personal prayer in a way that we can use just as effectively in our

119

very different world. The "feast" that was set before them was the daily reading, and it was served by the monk who could read. It was served slowly, with plenty of time for everyone to savor it.

As the listeners savored the reading, they were invited to choose any part of it that especially appealed to them and to take it away, in their minds and hearts, and chew it over in their cells. The chosen phrase or words then became the focus for a monk's private prayer and meditation.

Usually the day's Scripture would be read several times, and one by one the monks would disappear. Having found their "favorite chocolate," they would carry off their treasures to the privacy of their own cells to chew and digest the "Scripture filling." Until eventually there was no one left, and the reader could go to his own prayer.

Smorgasbord at the Dinorben Arms

A pub in North Wales called the Dinorben Arms always makes me think of this *lectio divina* prayer. They serve a "help yourself" lunch. There is a notice over the serving table inviting people to try a bit of everything and then come back for more of what they most enjoy. This is quite a good way of looking at chocolate-box prayer. We read, or listen to, a passage of Scripture and try each word, each phrase, as it slowly passes before us. And when we find a phrase, a thought, an image, or a memory that moves us in some way, we hold onto it and let that become our prayer.

You could compare it to browsing through a vacation brochure and letting your attention settle on a place that appeals to you. You see the picture and read the details, and something about that particular place attracts you. You might make a note of it and show it to your family. Together you might decide to give it a try and book a week at the resort. Then you will find out just what promise it held for you, and whether that promise is fulfilled in reality. Your instinctive feeling about the place is tested out by *living out* the experience of being there. In chocolate-box prayer, hearing or reading the Scripture passage is like browsing the brochure. Taking that phrase into your personal prayer is like experiencing the holiday.

There is no need at this stage to ask why this particular phrase is speaking to you or to try to analyze your reaction — in fact, to do so would be a distraction and an effort of the head instead of a response of the heart. Your subconscious mind is registering an interest in this word or image before your conscious mind has had a chance to get in the way. Like a buyer at an auction sale, your subconscious mind, guided by the Holy Spirit, raises a finger, as it were, to say, "I'll have that please." It is the same kind of spontaneous response you might feel when looking at a sunset. You might want for nothing more than simply to gaze and to let the beauty soak down into your being.

This kind of attentiveness automatically leads you to reflect on your experience and to respond to it in ways that will live on long after the time of prayer is over.

When you have chosen your phrase, savor it. Let God reveal its particular mystery for you. And then take it home. Where and how does it connect to your everyday life? How does it fit into the real world? Trust that God will speak to you through that word, phrase, or image. You may, for example, find yourself remembering a time when you have had similar feelings to those the phrase evokes in you. Were they feelings of delight or pain? Perhaps the phrase will challenge you or affirm you, question or comfort you. Whatever is happening, receive it as a gift from the Lord.

And so, your phrase has become a gateway to an encounter with the Lord. Let this encounter proceed in whatever way suggests itself. Ask God, as a child might ask a parent, to show you what God wants to show you through this prayer.

Finally, bring your prayer to a close by thanking God for the gifts he is bestowing deep in your heart in ways that lie beyond your knowledge or imagination. And, as with any kind of personal prayer, it is good to reflect afterwards, perhaps with a trusted friend, on what exactly held your attention so strongly, and why.

And the great thing is that taking the biggest chocolate in the box doesn't deprive anyone else of *her* favorite! Far from being a selfish activity, the prayer that takes you deeper into yourself is also taking you further into a communion where we are truly all one. What is healed in *you* is healed, in some mysterious way, for *all* the human family. What releases joy in you increases the joy of all.

Packed-Lunch Prayer

Perhaps I can share with you a particular way in which the prayer of *lectio divina* can provide a quick snack in a busy day.

It was during the school holidays, and we had visitors staying. Work was pressing, and my quiet space seemed quite inaccessible. I was missing the time of quiet in the early morning, yet there seemed no chance at all to carve out the space and solitude from the demands of those around me. One morning I was longing for a return to my routine, but it seemed like just another struggle for space and time. Eventually, however, I snatched a sacred five minutes on my own in a quiet corner. It was just long enough to ask God for the grace of peace and light and to read the daily readings. Nothing more.

A line in the psalm held my attention: "Instead of your ancestors you will have sons" (Psalm 45:16).

There was no time to meditate on it, but I knew it was speaking to me about freedom from inherited "baggage" and fruitfulness in an unknown future. Freedom and fruitfulness. I seized the crust of prayer gratefully; as I did so, I could hear God speaking somewhere inside me: *Packed-lunch prayer, to keep you going through a busy day. Have a nibble whenever you feel soul-hungry. Take this phrase out and feed on it whenever you have a moment's peace.*

And I knew that I had been given food for the day's journey — not a three-course meal but a nourishing packed lunch.

For this approach to prayer, you can use any passage that attracts and draws you. You can also use nonscriptural material (such as poems) in the same way, or you can let a visual image or painting speak its personal meanings to you by noticing the details that draw your attention and then taking them into prayer. In chocolate-box prayer we simply trust that God will speak to us, *whatever* raw materials we use to focus our hearts on him.

❦ TAKING IT FURTHER ❦

Find the chocolate

Using one of the stillness exercises we have been practicing — or any other way of coming to stillness that you find comfortable — relax and ask God for the gift of prayer. Ask God to open your heart to the personal meaning of the words you will read.

Then read a passage of Scripture (maybe the daily lectionary reading or any passage that appeals to you or draws your attention) slowly and reflectively, noticing every word, every phrase, every sentence. If any word or phrase seems to hold your attention or triggers feelings in you, either negative or positive, store it away in your memory.

Now reread the passage slowly, as if you were searching. If the same word or phrase catches your attention, stop your reading and try to sink into prayer, taking your phrase with you. Otherwise, keep on rereading the passage until you find your chocolate.

Once you have your phrase, let it hover there in your prayer, connecting you to God. For this prayer time, your phrase will be your prayer guide and director. Take note of whatever memories, feelings, or scenes it evokes in you. These images and promptings rise into consciousness from your own hidden depths, called up by the word that you have chosen. Allow them to emerge, unrestricted and unrepressed.

Do these memories, images, or feelings connect to anything that is happening in your life at present? If so, you might let your prayer become a conversation with the Lord. Tell God how you are feeling. Relive the memories with Jesus alongside you. Express your joy, anger, frustration, confusion, uncertainty. If the passage opens up doubts for you, don't be afraid to say, "But Lord, it isn't like that for *me!*" Expressing a doubt in this way is often a first step to reaching a more mature layer of trust. Or it may be a way of clearing your mind of issues that seem to be clouding your vision but are, in fact, not important to your deeper quest for God. No one can predict where such a personal prayer encounter will lead. But you can *trust*.

ADDITIONAL READING

Too Deep for Words: Rediscovering Lectio Divina, by Thelma Hall (Mahwah, N.J.: Paulist Press, 1988).

16

Meditating the Gospels Imaginatively

Can our imagination be a gateway to God?

✳

> *Prayer then is the interiorizing of the Incarnation.*
> *The Word is to become enfleshed in me. Bethlehem*
> *is here. So Christmas Day is to become all days,*
> *and the adoration of Emmanuel, God with us, must*
> *be a daily and continuous event.*
>
> — KENNETH LEECH, *TRUE PRAYER*

Can *my* imagination have any valid place in my prayer?" This might well be your first reaction to the suggestion that imagination has any place in a Christian's life of prayer. And your second reaction might be a more basic objection: "But I don't even have any imagination."

Let's deal with the second objection first. Have you ever waved good-bye to a loved one after a holiday — perhaps seen your son or daughter off to college or taken leave of your grandchildren after a midterm break or taken a friend to the airport — and then, for days afterwards perhaps, found yourself wondering what he would be doing right now and imagining his new surroundings? Or have you ever come home from a particularly memorable vacation and kept thinking back to the place and the people, imagining what you might be doing if you were there again?

If you can answer yes, then you cannot claim to have no imagination. And, more than that, you know how to use it to *reconnect* yourself to people and places you have loved but that are now
out of physical reach.

If you still think you don't have any imagination, just shut your
eyes for a moment and think of the sound of a person belly-flopping
into a swimming pool. Did you find yourself wincing inwardly?
Did your memory fly back briefly to the summer days of childhood? Or can you bring to mind the sickening thud of two cars in
collision? If so, what feelings does that memory evoke in you?

Imagination is part of the standard equipment that comes with
the mind and heart. And we use our imaginations in all kinds of
ways that we are probably unaware of. For now, let us just go
back to that kind of imagining that we might do after a memorable vacation — the kind of imagining that reconnects us to people and places we have come to love.

This kind of imagining can become a gateway to prayer. If we
can connect ourselves inwardly to other people and places, we
can use the same approach to become connected in a special and
conscious way to Jesus and to his earthly living, dying, and rising.
Jesus the man, who lived in Palestine two thousand years ago, is
physically out of reach. But our imaginations, used alongside the
Gospels, can draw us into a personal encounter with him, with
as much power to transform us as it did for the friends who accompanied the human Jesus all those centuries ago.

The only way to test this out is to try it for yourself. If you find it
helpful, it may become a powerful way of prayer for you. But, like
every other approach, it is only one way to pray, and not *the* way.

Where Two Worlds Meet

Imaginative prayer takes hold of both these facts:

- It *is* amazingly powerful to be present to the Lord in the events
of the Gospels.

- He *is* present to us where we are now, in our daily lives.

Your imagination can become the place where these two worlds meet: the world of Gospel reality and the world of your daily life.

To pray in this way, all you need to do is choose a Gospel story that especially appeals to you (one of the healing miracles, for example). There is no need to agonize over which passage to use. God can speak to your heart through any passage. Begin, as always, by asking God to be your guide and to give you the gift of prayer. Trust that whatever your imagination brings up will be enlightened by the gift of the Holy Spirit. Now simply relax, maybe close your eyes or focus on some steady object such as a candle or a flower, and let yourself imagine what the scene is like.

This is a very passive exercise. Try not to let yourself be seduced into making an effort. This isn't a test of your powers of descriptive writing or painting. It is simply the completely passive state of *letting yourself notice the pictures in your mind.* The scene that suggests itself to you may appear to have nothing remotely to do with the Palestine of two thousand years ago. This doesn't matter. What matters is what your unconscious mind is offering up for your attention. Just notice the scene, without attempting to stage manage it.

You may like to use some of these questions as a framework for your exploration of the scene you have chosen:

- What can I see, hear, smell, taste, feel?

- What is the weather like? Warm, cold, windy, peaceful, wet, dry?

- What seems to be happening in the scene? Who is here? Anyone I recognize?

- What kind of atmosphere does the scene suggest? Inviting, threatening, vibrant, solemn?

- Does any particular part of the scene attract my attention more than the rest of the scene?

Entering the Action

So far, you have set the scene. Whatever is there has arrived via your own imagination, under the guidance of God, in whom your prayer is firmly rooted.

You might compare this process with the way you look at the opening scene of a play. The curtain rises, and a scene is revealed in which the action will take place. In the theater or the cinema, you know nothing yet of how the action will work itself out or what the characters will be like. And this is how it is at the beginning of your imaginative prayer. You have read the script, certainly, and you are perhaps even overfamiliar with the events of the Gospel passage you have chosen, but what about *your* part in it? Powerful drama has the effect of drawing the audience into its own life and of *changing* the way they see and feel things in the future. And as Christians we believe that the Gospel is the most powerful drama there is. Will you leave that drama on the pages of your Bible, or will you risk entering the action?

To enter into the Gospel in your prayer requires a leap of faith because, however familiar you may be with the stories on which you are focusing, you cannot begin to predict what will happen when you get up from your comfortable front theater seat and walk onto the stage. The whole perspective changes. Suddenly you have a role in the drama. Simply by being there, you have become part of the action. You have stepped into the *present moment* of the drama, and you have surrendered the security of knowing the beginning, middle, and end of it. You are in the middle of it yourself, and it is happening around you.

When you reach this stage of your imaginative prayer, you might find some of these questions helpful.

- Where do I find myself? Am I one of the crowd? One of the disciples? Am I an outsider, a bystander looking on, or am I the person being healed or challenged or invited into a new relationship with Jesus? (Don't make any judgments or try to force yourself to be where you think you *ought* to be. The power of this kind of prayer is in being where you "find" yourself and letting the Gospel light shine on that place.)

- How am I feeling about what is happening in this scene? Disturbed? Attracted? Curious? Afraid? Eager?

- Do I feel drawn to speak with anyone here? What do I want to say? What do I feel is being said to me? Can I enter into a conversation with Jesus?

If you noticed earlier that one part of the scene drew you more powerfully than any other, let yourself go there now. Without forcing anything against your inclination, identify what is attracting you in that part of the scene.

If you feel able to do so, end your prayer by entering into a conversation with Jesus or perhaps with one of the disciples or with Mary (see chapter 17). Simply express your feelings about the experience and let your heart be open to receive whatever God may want to suggest to you. When you are ready, close your prayer in whatever way you find most helpful and spend a few minutes in reflection (see chapter 4).

How Do I Know This Is Prayer?

We cannot bypass the question with which this chapter began: Can my own imagination have any valid place in my prayer? Most of us tend to distrust our imagination. We regard it as the stuff of fairy tales, not to be indulged beyond childhood. We suspect that it is only one step short of deception. Our children tell us of some great dream they cherish or of some terror that haunts them, and we dismiss it with the words: "You're only imagining it." Or perhaps we confide in a friend some deep desire, only to have it shrugged off with a smile and, "Dream on!"

Yet the longer I live, the more I become convinced that my imagination is a God-given gateway to prayer, a place where I meet God in ways with which my busy conscious mind cannot interfere.

When I think of my own relationship with my imagination, I see an ocean, with boats busily plying to and fro, running my life's errands and trading for my bread and butter. How easily I can stay up there on the surface of myself, managing the traffic of my boats and forming alliances with the islands and continents that I can see around me. But if I ever stop to wonder what is in the depths beneath me, I might feel drawn to put on a diving suit and go have a look. I might find a whole, undiscovered world down there. There may be sharks, but there will be shoals of exquisitely beautiful fish as well. The imagination is like that underwater world. It can take us below our normal conscious functioning and show us something of the desires we may not realize we have.

It reminds me of the day when Jesus and Peter were confronted by the tax man demanding to know whether they thought they were required to pay the local tax. Jesus sent Peter to catch a fish from the lake and look into its mouth (Matthew 17:24–27), where he would find the necessary coin to pay the tax for both of them. Imaginative prayer sometimes feels like that for me. I meet the Lord in the Gospel, and he tells me to go down into the images I find in my own imagination. He invites me to take hold of these images, just as they come, as Peter caught hold of the first fish that swam past. If I look into these images, or into my own imagined reactions to a particular Gospel scene, I will find their meaning for me. This "coin" may reveal to me a new layer of understanding — of myself, my desires, and God's desires for me.

Let me share with you a shortened version of a personal encounter with Jesus in imaginative prayer. The scene of this particular prayer was the wedding at Cana (John 2:1–11).

> I felt oddly out of place at the wedding feast. I couldn't find the right kind of contact with the party goers. I suppose I just wasn't in a party mood. It was a hot summer day. Everybody was outside in the field. Most people were sitting at the tables, eating and drinking. I suddenly felt very shy and lonely. I was standing quite close to you and your disciples. It felt a bit safer like that. There I could hear what passed between you and your mother. "They've run out of wine," she said. It seemed obvious to her that you could solve the problem.
>
> You had been enjoying the festivities, and I could see that the unexpected challenge upset you. You were quite sharp with her. It was as though you had come to an abrupt turning point in your life and it had shaken the ground beneath you. I felt disturbed by the incident, but I could strongly identify with you. That particular moment seemed to reflect a sense of disorientation in my own life.

Were you reading my thoughts? What made you come over to me the way you did? "There has been a running out for you too, hasn't there?" you asked me, quietly, so that no one else could hear.

I nodded, surprised that you should be able to see inside me so clearly.

"Come with me," you said. I followed you as you walked, pensively, a little further away from the party crowd. I let you walk ahead. I could see that you needed space for yourself.

Mary walked beside me unobtrusively. "Don't worry," she re-assured me. "Just do as he tells you."

We passed by the six stone water jars. I barely noticed them. The servants were filling them up with water from the nearby well, but it was an everyday scene. You stopped to ask one of the servants to draw off a carafe of water from one of the jars and take it over to the host. I noticed the rich crimson wine running into the carafe, but even then the nature of what had happened didn't sink in.

You sat down on a boulder at the edge of the field and beck-oned me to join you. We sat there together in silence for a while. I closed my eyes against the dazzling sunlight and let my thoughts trickle away into the grass, like water draining away from an over-turned pitcher. Eventually I had emptied myself into the silence that enclosed us. I felt drained and sad for the emptying. Yet there was a cleansing in the empty space. It had been a necessary emp-tying. What had been there could not have stayed longer.

I was reminded of my own child's birth. I remembered that strange vacuum I had experienced when what I had carried was no longer in me. The sense of a dramatic passage from an old to a new creation. I remembered the complete exhaustion that followed, and I felt something of the same exhaustion there beside you on the rock, in the afternoon heat. At my child's birth, the midwife had moved a fan close to my forehead. Now, here with you, a gentle breeze brushed my brow, and I knew it had to do with you. You were assisting at a birth, yet not a word was spoken.

My memories returned to the labor ward and slid softly through the first hours of the baby's life. With vivid recollection I experienced again that tingling sensation that signaled that my body was ready to feed its firstborn. I looked up at you, and you were gazing steadily into my face. I heard again your words to the servant: "Draw off a carafe of water and take it to the guests." But this time the words thrilled me with the full sense of miracle. I re-membered how, with a surge of love, I had taken my daughter in my arms, and with her tiny mouth she had drawn her first nourish-ment from me. My drained, exhausted, empty body of yesterday had become a source of life and growth for the newborn. I had done nothing, felt nothing, yet overnight an amazing transformation had occurred, and the life-giving milk flowed out of emptiness.

That had been many years ago, but here in the sunlit field it had returned to me as if I were reliving it. I moved closer to you, to thank you, to kneel before you in recognition of who you are. You stroked my bowed head. "And so it is with the water of your soul," you whispered softly. "You didn't do anything. You didn't notice anything. But in the silence and the emptiness, your Creator was making all things new. At first the transformation remains a secret. The water jar does not know what it contains, and the world cannot guess. But the day comes, for you too, when I invite someone to draw from you a carafe of needed refreshment, and the water is found to be the finest wine. The miracle is recognized only when the wine is drawn. If it stays in the jar, it might just as well be water, but if it is drawn off and shared, it will bring joy and the fullness of life.

We walked back across the field together, side by side, in comfortable companionship, and I understood the heart of the feasting and rejoiced in the richness of the promised vintage.

We began this whole exploration of personal prayer by considering the need to focus our hearts toward God in some particular way. The way of imaginative prayer is one way to practice this focusing, but it does more than that; it draws together two different but connected stories — the Gospel story you are imagining and your own personal story. This has the effect of bringing the two into a single focus, so that the Gospel light and the light of Jesus' living presence shine upon your own experience in very specific detail. The results of this focusing may challenge you to the core, but they will also bring you joy, a new depth of friendship with God, and a fuller understanding of what it might mean for you to become more alive in him.

A Prayer — or a Daydream?

And how do I know (for example in the prayer encounter I have described), that this was prayer and not just a daydream? I would suggest these ways of testing your prayer experience and discerning what is of God and what is merely a passing fantasy.

• What comes from God will last and will bring about real change within you. The Cana prayer experience described above is well over six years old now, but I remember it as vividly as if it were yesterday. It has become part of who I am. It has changed my perspective on things, especially when I am feeling drained, and it continues to give me a vision of the power that is released when we are poured out.

• What comes from God has a peculiar characteristic of weaving itself, seamlessly, into our personal experience and our memories. In the Cana prayer, I trust you can almost feel the Lord's fingers picking up the threads of my feelings of desolation and my memories of childbirth and folding them into his own experience of challenge and hesitation when the wine ran out at the wedding. In authentic imaginative prayer, there is a consistency between our own experience and God's self-revelation. There is a kind of oneness between the way he reveals himself in the Gospel narrative and the way he reveals himself through the windows of our memory and the images that arise from our subconscious minds. It can feel almost like reading a parallel text translation of an ancient classic. We read the original text in the pages of the Gospel, and alongside it, intertwined with it, we read our own memories and experience.

• What comes from God will draw us closer to him and closer to one another, though it may lead us through hard challenges. What comes only from ourselves will tend to focus on ourselves, and lead us further away from God and from one another. An encounter with God leaves us with an awareness of a movement toward life and growth, which self-focused pondering can never yield.

Some questions, then, to ask yourself:

• Has my prayer made any difference to the way I am?

• Is my prayer consistent with what else is happening in my life?

• Does my prayer lead me closer to God and to other people?

• Is my center of gravity now beyond myself, in God and in God's creation?

If you can answer these questions positively, then you can be assured that your prayer was more than just a flight of fantasy. If there are good fruits, they have come from a sound tree. All you need to do is to give that tree the time and space to grow in your heart and allow the fruits time to ripen.

All through this chapter we have concentrated mainly on the use of imagination to enter the Gospel scenes. Your imagination can, however, be used very powerfully on any passage of Scripture, or you may find it helpful to pray imaginatively with non-scriptural material. Many people find that a picture or a piece of poetry can open up unconscious streams within them and lead them into the communion of prayer. Others discover a key to their inner world in fantasy prayer, simply by allowing an image (perhaps of a tree or a remembered scene) to form freely in their minds and then following in prayer wherever it leads them.

And if you are one of those people who remember their dreams, you have another rich vein of treasure accessible to you. Notice your dreams, especially what some people call big dreams — the kind of dream that stays with you long after you dream it. I have often found that such dreams have helped me become aware of hitherto unrecognized areas and layers of my being. Such dreams have become an ongoing prayer within me and have continued to release guiding and transforming power.

My Light or God's?
An Exercise in Discernment

Prayer brings light. Jesus said he was the Light of the world, and this is the light we seek in prayer. How do we know, when we think that there has been enlightenment in our prayer, that the light is really God's and not merely our own?

The following guidelines might help us be discerning.

- The light that comes from God makes a difference. God's light is similar to the sun's light. It generates and sustains life; it keeps us warm; it makes us grow; it provides energy we can feel, trust, and use. When we follow it, we *know* that we are being enlivened.

- Our own lights — our intellectual sparks and bright ideas — may dazzle, but they will not leave us with inner warmth. They will not bring about any true growth or change in us. In their effects our own lights remain cold and without the power of miracle.

My own lights, I find, may momentarily illuminate a part of my tangle of experience, but they will fade as soon as my battery runs low. God's light enlivens all creation. It sustains us and forms us, even as we grope around in darkness.

❈ TAKING IT FURTHER ❈

An experiment in imaginative prayer

Try to imagine a scene that happened just a short time before Jesus entered the final, terrible week of his life. He is visiting friends in Bethany, not far from Jerusalem — Martha, Mary, and Lazarus, together with some of his disciples, including Judas. Not long before he had raised Lazarus from the dead, and this had attracted the attention of the authorities. Lazarus' journey back to life had become the immediate cause of Jesus' being sentenced to death. Perhaps, as they share this meal together, the four friends are somehow aware of these connections — of the joy at Lazarus' return to life, of the wonder at the power in the hands and the heart of their friend Jesus, and of a vague apprehension, a dull fear of the darkness looming ahead of them.

Before you begin your prayer, read through the passage where this scene is described. You may feel drawn to read it through several times, letting the feel of it sink in. Read slowly, as if soaking up the atmosphere of the place and the feelings of the people.

> Six days before the Passover, Jesus went to Bethany, where Lazarus was, whom he had raised from the dead. They gave a dinner for him there; Martha waited on them and Lazarus was among those at table. Mary brought in a pound of very costly ointment, pure nard, and with it anointed the feet of Jesus, wiping them with her hair; the house was filled with the scent of the ointment. Then Judas Iscariot — one of the disciples, the man who was to betray him — said, "Why was this ointment not sold for three hundred denarii and the money given to the poor?" He said this, not because he cared about the poor, but because he was a thief; he was in charge of the common fund and used to help himself to the contents. So Jesus said, "Leave her alone; let her keep it for the day of my burial. You have the poor with you always, you will not always have me."
> Meanwhile a large number of Jews heard that he was there and came not only on account of Jesus but also to see Lazarus whom he had raised from the dead. Then the chief priests decided to kill Lazarus as well, since it was on his account that many of the Jews were leaving them and believing in Jesus.
>
> (John 12:1 – 11)

Imagine the place where this scene is happening. How does the room look and feel? Notice the details that come to mind — the shape and size of the room, the furniture, windows, and views out of those windows.

Who is in the room? Where are you? Take time to notice everything about the place; see the colors and listen to whatever sounds you can hear — sounds outside and inside the house. Notice any scents — perhaps the smell of cooking or the fragrance of flowers. Use all your senses to re-create the scene as it feels right for you.

How do you feel in that scene — comfortable, peaceful, disturbed? Don't make any judgments or try to work out reasons for your feelings. Just let them be there and become aware of them.

Now turn your attention to the people in the scene. What are they doing? Are any conversations taking place? What is the underlying mood of these conversations? Do you feel drawn to join in any of them? What, if anything, do you feel you would like to say? If you could interview one of them, who would it be? Feel free to go up to that person and express whatever it is that you would like to say or ask. Do you feel drawn to speak to Jesus in a personal way? Let this conversation take its course. Speak to him of whatever is in your heart, and listen to his response. Notice the look on his face (if you can) and the tone of his voice. In a significant meeting with a friend, you would be very observant of the body language and the unspoken feelings passing between you. Do the same now with Jesus, if you feel drawn to do so.

You might like to let your imagination roam over one or both of the central events of the scene. Mary comes into the room carrying a container of precious ointment to pour over Jesus' feet. Imagine her feelings as she does so. How do *you* feel? (For example, some people may feel drawn to make their own offering of what is most precious to them; others may feel aloof and distant from the action, or embarrassed or disturbed. Don't *judge* your reaction, simply notice it.) Judas objects to what he regards as a waste. Listen to his reaction and notice how *you* feel. Do either of these two incidents pick up any memories in you, reminding you of anything in your own life? Just notice which, if either, draws you into it. Notice your own role in all of this: maybe as an observer, not involved, or perhaps you find yourself identifying with Mary, Martha, Lazarus, Judas, one of the disciples, or Jesus himself. *Anything* can happen in imagination: don't put up any resistance to whatever floats up into your scene, even if you feel that it isn't the right way to respond. There is no right or wrong way in prayer. Whatever is happening in your prayer has something to show you about your relationship with God and his movement in your heart.

If you are comfortable with this kind of prayer, it can help you discover a great deal about what is happening between you and God in the depths of your heart. But this will only be helpful if, after a period of prayer, you spend a few minutes *reflecting* on it (see chapter 4).

Let's suppose, for example, that you felt quite remote from Mary and her act of anointing, but Judas's words made you sit up and take notice. What caused that change in your level of attention?

Anger with Judas, perhaps, or impatience with Mary, or what? Ponder what your findings may be showing you — about yourself or your situation, about any agenda important to you right now.

Look back especially over any conversations you had in your prayer. Just as you might review a conversation that happened at work or in the family, taking in what was said, how it was said, what the implications were, and so forth, so too you will find it helpful and revealing to look back at any prayer conversations, especially if you were able to speak to Jesus.

ADDITIONAL READING

Six New Gospels, by Margaret Hebblethwaite (Boston: Cowley, 1994).

Imagine That! by Marlene Halpin (Roa, Iowa: W. C. Brown, 1982).

17

Conversing through Prayer

Between friends

※

Once I heard someone say that the Chinese search for
the jade ring through which they can speak to God and
God to them. All of us are looking for our jade ring,
a place and perhaps a method for meeting God.
— WILLIAM BARRY, GOD AND YOU —
PRAYER AS PERSONAL RELATIONSHIP

Conversation is the most obvious way of developing friendship
in human relationships. If, in prayer, we are seeking a personal
relationship with God, then surely such a relationship would
grow and be expressed in the course of *conversation*. Does the
notion of holding a conversation with God make any sense in the
life of prayer?

In our human friendships, our conversations are not limited to
a single person. We hold conversations in different ways with different people. And our friendship with one particular person will
very often lead us to meet, and enter into relationship with, others.
We speak of a *circle of friends*. And we also frequently depict the
Trinity as a circle of unbroken relationship among the Father, the
Son, and the Holy Spirit. Can prayer lead us into the mystery of
this communion of friendship?

And can our conversations with God help us better understand
the unbroken networks of communication that hold our human
lives together? Will conversing with God help us tap into the inner

dialogue in which we are continually engaged between God's creation and our own senses? Will it help us make better sense of the outer dialogues we have with one another?

Finally, the difficult, yet unavoidable question: How can we be sure that it is God speaking to our hearts in prayer and not just some script that we have written for ourselves?

Conversations with God

What might it mean to enter into a conversation with God? Isn't it a bit like trying to use a transistor radio to tune in to the meaning of the universe? Isn't a conversation with God just a rather inflated way of describing what is really a conversation with ourselves?

In a way it is. But it is much more than that. Through prayer we enter conversations that are in one sense merely a dialogue between our conscious and unconscious self. Yet we also believe — and I think we know — that there is something, Someone, much greater than our mere selves at the heart of ourselves. We believe that our innermost center is mysteriously and eternally connected to the heart of all that is — whom we call God. When we pray, we believe that it is the Holy Spirit who prays in us, and that he fulfills his promise to draw this hidden center of ourselves into the heart of God. Prayer rests on this trust.

Do such conversations have any real value, or are they just a pious pastime? What might be going on when we talk to God about what is on our minds? In an attempt to answer this question, I invite you to judge for yourself as you read the following snippet of one such conversation of mine. In this example, I had been meditating on the fall and on Adam's judgment — to till the soil from which God had created him. To me it seemed like a sentence to a long term in a labor camp, doing work that appeared to have no results.

> I: "Prayer takes me back to Eden this morning. I feel as if I am standing in the courtroom, all my untruth exposed to you, and waiting for your verdict. You begin to speak. You tell me that I must till the ground from which you took me, just as you did yourself."

JESUS: "I tilled the ground where I found myself—the ground out of which the Father created my earthly being."

I: "It sometimes seems so pointless, Lord. Like struggling to solve a problem, knowing very well that a similar problem will come back again tomorrow."

JESUS: "It often seemed pointless to me too. My family and neighbors would never take me seriously and I often doubted even myself. And *was* it pointless?"

I: "What can I say? Here we are, two thousand years later, knowing that we *know* you. But even now, knowing your risen life, we seem to make so little impact anywhere. A small group of people gathers, listens, prays, grows, and then disperses, without apparently having had much effect."

JESUS: "A small group gathers, listens, prays, grows, and then disperses—exactly the pattern of my own life. So why do you keep on tilling?"

I: "It's the only way I can stay true to myself."

JESUS: "And so it was for me."

I: "Tilling means staying precisely here, with the soil from which you took me."

JESUS: "And tilling means coaxing, not bullying. Gently urging the earth into freedom and fruitfulness."

I: "And if the squirrels keep digging up my bulbs?"

JESUS: "Keep planting more. And pray for the squirrels."

I: "And I see, this morning, that your commandment to till the ground is not a punishment, but a call to share in your work of redemption and healing and restoration."

Notice in this snippet how the imagined words of Jesus work as a wise soul friend might; they reflect back to me what is really coming from my heart and my desire. They bring me up against challenging questions about what I really want. And they point me to parallels in Jesus' own life that are obvious once they are pointed out, and which encourage and strengthen me. Though, psychologically speaking, they are coming from my own psyche, spiritually they are also coming from the Holy Spirit, who works in me through my mental and psychological processes, my experience and memories and emotions, to show up the dark and light patches in me and lead me forward, growing. You could even compare such a conversation (and indeed all forms of personal prayer) with an X-ray exposure. It shows up parts of myself that cannot readily be seen in everyday consciousness.

So don't be afraid to engage in conversation with the Lord. (This is more formally called a colloquy.) You can pour out whatever you are feeling and know that he will receive it in love and compassion. You can express your anger with him. He is more than big enough to take it! But listen to his side of the dialogue too. It might surprise you! And sometimes this element of startling and joyous surprise can be a hallmark of the authenticity of your prayer. You may find yourself exclaiming, from time to time: "I don't know where that came from; it's the last thing I would have said myself." Let such surprises both delight and enlighten you. They come from depths of yourself that only God has fathomed, and they are true gift.

Meeting New Friends

It would be a strange kind of friendship that never introduced the friend to other friends and family. Going home to meet the relatives can be daunting in human life, but it is a vital part of a friendship's development. We know that friendship rarely survives in isolation. As I write, we have a young Hungarian guest staying with us for a couple of weeks to learn the language and see something of our country. When asked what she would especially like to do, she said that, among other things, she would like to meet our daughter's friends. And what could be more natural than to introduce a new friend to our old friends?

Yet it seemed strange to me at first that God might want to introduce me to some of his other friends. And the difference with God is that his friends may be found anywhere, among the living and the dead, the saints and the sinners, the past and the present. We are in for some surprises when God takes us to meet the family!

When God introduces us to his friends, we can find ourselves in a kind of three-dimensional conversation, or, as it is called more formally in some traditions, a triple colloquy. Such a conversation often begins with some human member of the communion of saints (Mary, for example), who then leads us to Jesus, who in turn takes us to the Father. This is a very valuable way of deepening prayer and allowing it to lead us gently from our personal history into God's mystery.

An example may help to illustrate the dynamic of such a conversation.

I woke up just after 5 A.M. and felt as if the night were over. Something seemed to call me to you and to prayer. All I could say was, "You called me, Lord; here I am."

I brought myself to stillness; it didn't seem so difficult in this borderland between sleep and consciousness. The darkness and the silence held no distractions. Strange, how the darkness can clarify one's vision.

I let my prayer take the form of a triple colloquy. I searched for Mary. I found her in her little house in the village. It felt like seeking out an older, wiser friend, who could lead me to you, Lord. She welcomed me and drew me into her home. We talked for a while. Then she invited me to visit her garden.

The garden was an open space right in the center of her house, alive with water, leaping up in fountains and flowing down in waterfalls. I knew that was the living Water, and that she was answering my prayer to lead me to you.

Some of the fountains were leaping high and strong. I thought of some of the people I know in whom the living Water rises in a surge. Other fountains were just gurgling, and some were totally stopped. And the waterfalls seemed like a flow of grace coming down from all those who have gone before us.

"If you are looking for my Son," Mary said, "he is over there." I saw the figure of a man kneeling on the ground beside one of the fountains. It was one of the weaker ones, and he was gently unclogging it with his fingers. His whole attention was focused on the clogged-up fountain. I knew that it was you. I watched your face as you worked. There was no reproach, no blame, no anger. Only tenderness, and an overriding desire to free the fountain into life again.

You welcomed me silently, not interrupting your work, yet holding me too in your attention. I knew that what you were doing for that little fountain you were also doing for me and my clogged-up heart. I begged you to do it, even if it meant using a steel brush on me sometimes (and it has!), because the desire of my fountain to flow free was so much more powerful than anything else.

"Let me take you to the Father," you said, turning your gaze toward me. I wondered, apprehensively, where and how the Father might be, and whether he would accept me. Then you took my hand, and together we seemed to sink down into the infinite source of the Water that was feeding all the fountains. I knew that my deepest desire had found its source. And, amazingly, when you took me to the Father, I knew where I was! It felt like a homecoming.

Yet even as I touched the heart of the mystery, my own heart was darkened by the knowledge of the untruth and the sin that clogs the outflow of your love through me. My heart darkened and the vision faded. Yet the vision is not lost, because you are always there, kneeling beside the failing springs, searching out the source of all our obstructions. Again, you turned toward me, your face alight with love. "The hands of my friends will do this work as well," you told me. "They will tend the failing springs in others, nurturing the renewal of their flow. This is how to set the captives free and to unbind what is bound. This is the whole desire of the Father, to express his love in every human life, and this is our task, the task of us all together, to dissolve everything that obstructs that flow, by touching it with love."

Listening to Our Senses

We know that human conversations (and even communications among other creatures) depend heavily on body language. So much of what we communicate to one another is not expressed in words at all but in our unconscious gestures, movements, tones of voice, or other physical signals. We speak to one another constantly by means of body language, and we receive these signals from one another through our five senses.

Such dialogue, being independent of words, can exist between people who have no knowledge of the other's language. It can even exist between human beings and animals, as anyone who owns a pet will testify. So surely God, too, will use our bodily senses as gateways through which to communicate with our hearts.

Consider this prayer conversation I had with the three Persons of the Trinity:

FATHER: "I created your eyes, that you might see all that I have created."
SON: "I opened your eyes, so that you might see the hidden mystery of things."
HOLY SPIRIT: "I am the Light, that reveals all this to you."

FATHER: "I created your ears, that you might hear the sound of my creation: its songs and its cries, its power and its subtlety."
SON: "I opened your ears, so that you might respond to the crying and the laughter of creation."
HOLY SPIRIT: "I am the empty space, where sound resounds."

FATHER: "I created your taste buds, so that you might taste all the flavors of my creation."
SON: "I opened up your taste buds to respond to sweet and bitter, fresh and stale."
HOLY SPIRIT: "I am the discernment guiding you to choose what is wholesome and leave aside what is harmful to you."

FATHER: "I created your nose, so that you might receive all the signals of scent that my creation produces."
SON: "I opened up your sense of smell, so that you might respond to the scents of life and turn from those of death."
HOLY SPIRIT: "I am the attraction drawing you to the scents of growth and life, of flowers, fruit and fresh summer mornings, of salt spray and new-mown hay and baking bread and rising yeast. I am the Warning who repels you from the stench of death and staleness and rot and waste and all that corrodes and pollutes."

FATHER: "I created your nerves, your skin, your fingertips, so that you might have feeling for my creation."
SON: "I opened up your sense of touch, and turned it into sensitivity, knowing both pain and pleasure."

HOLY SPIRIT: "I am the tenderness that exposes your heart to the overflow of love and the stabs of pain. For tenderness carries both, knows both, unites both in the mystery of life and growth."

Three Persons and five senses and finally the encircling silence with which prayer begins and ends.

Healing Encounters

A rather special form of conversation with God can take the form of a three-way conversation in your imagination between yourself, Jesus, and another person who has hurt you or is for some reason estranged from you. Sometimes this kind of scenario can make it possible for you, with the Lord alongside, to face feelings that you would not be able to express in a real conversation with the person concerned.

Just let yourself be in a place, in your imagination, where you feel safe, and invite the Lord to be there with you, maybe telling him about the problem you have with this person. Then, when you feel ready, draw the person into the safe place with you, and express, through Jesus, what you are feeling. Give the other person an opportunity to say how he or she is feeling about things. Finally, you might turn to Jesus and ask him to share his truth and his love with you both. Notice what suggests itself to you during this period of prayer. It may shed significant light on the difficulties and offer you a breakthrough in the deadlock.

Sometimes inner conversations of this nature, carried out in the privacy of your own prayer, can be extremely healing. Very often, however, it is advisable to explore the feelings that these encounters arouse in you with a trusted guide. I recall once opening up and reliving in prayer a painful memory and feeling almost overwhelmed by the anguish it evoked in me. This anguish might have become destructive, had I not been able to share the whole encounter with a trusted friend, who listened to my feelings and fears, helping me to notice where they were coming from and where they were leading. In this way, the two of us together, in the conscious presence of God, were able to discover creative ways of moving forward.

I believe, myself, that the Holy Spirit guides us only as far as we are ready to go. If prayer brings you up against a pain barrier that you feel uneasy about crossing alone, the time may be ripe for you to seek the right companion before you go any further.

If you find that serious traumatic memories are coming up for you in prayer, don't try to struggle with them alone, and don't be afraid to seek professional help from a therapist or a trained practitioner of healing prayer.

God Speaking?

We mustn't sidestep the big question: How do I know that this is God speaking to my heart and that this is not all my own mental script? This question should be asked of all that we call revelations or insights or enlightenments in prayer. How do we know when God is speaking?

In chapter 16 we looked at considerations in the context of imaginative meditation. These considerations also apply here. In short:

- What comes from God will stay with us, take root, grow, and eventually bear fruit. What comes only from ourselves and the mental scripts we write will not have a very long shelf life. Our own insights tend to fade.

- What comes from God will tend to turn our attention *away* from ourselves and toward God, his people, and his creation. What comes merely from ourselves will often be centered on ourselves and the furtherance of our own little kingdoms and agenda.

You will know a conversation by its fruits, but you will need to give those fruits time to ripen. One way of encouraging this ripening process is to practice deepening in on what seems to be most significant in our prayer, in the ways suggested in chapter 12.

Spiritual Conversations

And there are other conversations that we as Christians are urged to have. These are serious conversations with one another about our relationship with God.

We know that we are called to spread the gospel, and we may have widely differing views on how we can best do this in our particular circumstances. This is not a book about mission and evangelization in this particular sense, but there are two ways of entering into spiritual conversations with others that have a place in these reflections on meeting God in personal prayer:

- We can talk with a soul friend about our inner journeys, in the ways suggested in chapter 23. This is an invaluable way of deepening our relationship with God in the companionship of another believer who will listen to our stories and help us discern God's action in them.

- We can also listen to the stories of other people, without making any attempt to convert or correct them. This provides fertile soil in which the seed of their faith can take root and grow, and it is perhaps among the most valuable gifts that one human being can give to another.

❧ TAKING IT FURTHER ❧

Have a tea talk

If the idea of talking to God is new to you, try sitting down in your prayer space, maybe even with a cup of tea or coffee, and talking over the issues that concern you, just as you would with a friend. When you do this, take off your Sunday suit and just be yourself. Tell God exactly how you feel about things. Don't exclude describing emotions just because they're dark — anger, fear, or frustration.

Listen to a person

Take an opportunity to have an in-depth conversation with a friend or even with a person you may not know very well. As far as you both feel comfortable, try exploring what you are both about. This is as much an exercise in listening as in talking. A conversation of this kind is not an exercise in outreach or evangelization but a shared time of mutual discovery.

A triple colloquy

A friend, who had never heard of the triple colloquy and would probably not have felt drawn to practice it if she had, was meditating one day with a rather striking and unusual picture of (a modern) Mary sitting at the seashore, holding her child in her arms. The child Jesus is allowing himself to be held in her embrace but also straining toward something beyond it. He is reaching out his hand and pointing to a bright star in the sky.

The picture she was using is a triple colloquy in itself. The viewer's gaze is first drawn to Mary's face, full of love and trust yet also touched by sorrowful apprehension. Mary is gazing at her little Son, and our eyes are led by hers to him. She leads us, or introduces us, to him. He, in turn, is pointing to the stars and to all that is beyond, all that suggests the invisible origin of creation in the Father.

You might like to ponder my friend's response to this picture. Notice how she listens in, first to Mary's words to her Child, then to Mary's invitation to Jesus to talk to the Father about what he is seeing and feeling, and finally to the conversation Jesus tells her the Father has had with him and the peace-giving, trust-restoring effect in both their hearts.

Star of Wonder, Star of Joy

"Not now, my love, not yet,
You can run free when you're older,

Stay with me and come to bed
For the night is growing colder.
Yes, I know you want a star,
A brilliant, sparkly shining light,
And one day you will, my love,
And you'll make the world so bright.
You'll hold it in your hand,
Yes, for all the world to see;
No, I don't know how it'll happen
But I know that it will be.
So be patient, dearest love,
And make the most of having fun,
For the day will come to pass
When you will know you are God's Son.

"Pick your shells up now, my love,
We must go home right away,
Say good night to star of hope
Until your glory comes to stay.
We'll tell God all about it
When you're kneeling quiet to pray,
You can tell me what he says, Dear,
If he talks to you today."

"He says he loves us, Mother,
Not to worry, just to wait."
And she watched him fall asleep
And she pondered on his fate.
Such a joy was in her hands
Never failing to amaze
As she knelt beside his bed
Lost in wonder, love, and praise.

R. A. Hulme

18

Praying When Life Hurts

Between a rock and a hard place

*

*You can begin anytime, anywhere, even if you are only
a tiny grain of mustard seed lying in a pit of terror.*
— DONALD NICHOLL, *HOLINESS*

A pilgrim's first experience of personal prayer can feel like an entrance into a realm of pure joy. The sense of being drawn ever more closely to God is consoling, which, in its original sense, means being with the sun or in the presence of the Source and Sustainer of our being.

Yet inevitably our lives also include valleys of shadow and darkness, where we can almost forget that we ever felt the warmth of the sun in our hearts. When I find myself in the dark places, it's helpful to remember that God's presence in my life *is* like the sun — it is always there, upholding my existence with its never-failing energy, even when the clouds hide it and I can't feel its effects. God is the eternal reality *"in whom we live, and move and have our being"* (Acts 17:28 KJV), and the things in our lives that block our awareness of that eternal reality are only temporary. They do not have the final word. The clouds can block the sun for a while, but they have no power to destroy it.

Even so, the cloudy times can easily come to dominate us. Prayer that tries to skirt around the pain that overshadows so much of our human living can never be authentic. Where is God in those darknesses? Is there a place for prayer, or any point to prayer, when life is hurting?

151

The Rock . . .

Allow me to change metaphors. From shadows and clouds to "hitting a rock," slamming into a brick wall. The prophet Elijah spoke out to King Ahab of God's anger, and then Elijah hit a rock and had to flee into the desert (1 Kings 17:2–6). You might put yourself in Elijah's place for a few minutes, by becoming aware of any situation in your own life that feels like the rock. Perhaps a situation in which there seems to be no way forward, a relationship that causes you pain and shows no hope of any improvement, or a memory that holds you captive in resentment or fear. Let your personal circumstances show you your own desert, and spend a few minutes there with Elijah.

We find him in the middle of nowhere, in the Wadi Cherith, an exile and a frightened fugitive, full of doubts about his own mission and about God's fidelity, and close to starvation. Two chapters later he is again on the run, this time in suicidal despair, begging God to take his life.

Notice what happens in each of these situations. We are told two facts about Elijah in the Wadi Cherith: He drinks from a stream, and the ravens bring him bread in the morning and meat in the evening. Two chapters later we are told that out in the wilderness near Beersheba, the despairing prophet falls into an exhausted sleep, but an angel touches him and urges him to eat, to nourish himself. When he looks around, he finds a scone baked on hot stones and a jar of water; he eats and drinks.

I find these stories among the most encouraging in all the Scriptures, perhaps because I know, in my own small way, how it feels to be like Elijah on this hard rock. And there is something that rings true in my memory about that stream; about the food brought, apparently out of the blue, by the ravens; about the angel's touch and the unexpected meal, along with the gentle persuasion to take and eat.

I think that these pictures of Elijah's agony can bring us closer to an understanding of God's invisible presence in our own hard experiences. We can turn this story into something real and alive for ourselves if we can get in touch with the ways in which God does, or ever has done, something similar for us or for those we love. Try reflecting, for example, on the following:

- Times when you have been down and out and some little signal of encouragement came to you, perhaps from a totally unexpected source.

- Areas of your life that feel like deserts, with nothing to cheer or encourage you, but where, if you look back and look hard, you can see a tiny trickle of water that has somehow kept you going against the odds. What was, or is, that life-saving stream for you?

- Days, months, or years of despair that have been punctuated now and again by an angel's touch that restored your faith in yourself and in humanity. Who touched you then?

- Times when you have wound yourself down into exhaustion and maybe cried yourself to sleep, then awakened to find a renewed calm, a fresh perspective, new sustenance for tomorrow's journey. Not a banquet! Just a day's supply of baked scones and clear water. Just enough for one more step into the future. And a loving word that urges you to choose life by taking and eating. Who brought you that midnight feast, and how did you react?

All these little signs and wonders are the proof of God's presence and help for us at all times. Prayer can help us to take hold of these God-given life savers and let his strength sustain us. Prayer can also bring to our attention ways in which we might work with God in feeding others who have come to the end of their resources.

Prayer, if it is honest, does not deny the darkness in our hearts and the anguish in our lives, but it can lead us to streams in the desert and the morsels of food that we never expected. A very effective way to discover this water and bread or to become aware of the angel's touch is to stay faithful especially to those few minutes each day when we look back over the past twenty-four hours and notice where and how God has been with us. This can be the place in which we are enabled to do what Elijah did next: "He got up and ate and drank, and strengthened by that food he walked for forty days and forty nights until he reached Horeb, God's mountain" (1 Kings 19:8).

. . . and the Hard Place

The hardest place of all, in our human experience, is the Calvary place, the Gethsemane garden, where Jesus plumbed the depths of all human grief and despair. Can we ever connect to this kind of pain? If so, can it help us to understand and grow through our own?

We have looked, in chapter 16, at the possibility of praying the Gospel stories imaginatively. This kind of prayer can (and eventually *will*) lead us into an imaginative sharing of Jesus' last days on earth. And there it can reveal to us the very personal ways in which we play our own part in the events of those days. When we enter the scenes of Holy Week in our imagination, we are inviting the Lord to take us into the very heart of the matter. There, if we will let him, he will open up to us those ways in which our personal pain and grief connects to his and the way in which he, in his agony, is connecting to us in ours.

Some people find, for example, that they are standing alongside Pilate, washing their hands of responsibility in particular dilemmas that call for decisive commitment. Others, who maybe complain loudly about violence on the television screens or in the streets, discover to their shame that *they* are playing a part in the violence against Jesus. Some sense within themselves the instinct to run or to deny any knowledge of this hunted criminal who was once their friend. Then again, some people discover a powerful longing in their hearts to be with the Lord in his hours of agony, to follow him, to offer him the drink he asks for or to tend his broken body. There are endless possibilities; as always in this kind of prayer, you will not be able to predict where you will find yourself. From one day to another, your place in these events will change. And all the while you will be discovering things about yourself that you had perhaps not been aware of before.

In all of this, keep in mind Jesus' admonitions not to judge ourselves or others. And know that, with tenderness and with infinite love, God will lead you to where he wants you to be.

Most surely, aspects of your own self will cause you to grieve for your part in the world's Calvary. Just as surely, aspects of your own self will reveal your longing to be close to the Lord. Just let your prayer bring up for you those *particular* ways in which *your* experience of life, with its pain and its shame as well as its faithfulness and trust, connects to the experience of Jesus in his suffering and death.

Living your own hurts in the gospel light of Jesus' suffering has some important consequences:

- It shifts your focus away from the immediate pain in your own life and toward the even greater pain in *Jesus'* life and in his world's. This is the first movement toward healing, and the healing he is offering to you is not just for you but, in some mysterious way, for the entire human family. When your pain is joined with his, it becomes part of his redeeming love.

- It will lead you through dark Friday to resurrection Sunday, because, as we noticed earlier, the sun and not the clouds are the permanent reality. God's indestructible life, which permeates our human lives, is eternal, not our sin and brokenness.

How often have you heard this question asked or asked it yourself, in the face of some terrible disaster or painful, immovable blockage in your life: Where is God in this suffering?

If you have the courage in your personal prayer to enter into the suffering, death, and resurrection of the Lord, you may find his question answering your own: Where are *you* in mine? If you let him, he will gently show you where you are in his, and this will become a way in which he can open up your life to his healing.

Ground between the Stones

I have subtitled this chapter "Between a Rock and a Hard Place" because something very creative can happen when we find ourselves crushed between two overwhelming forces.

Sometimes it can feel that we are being ground into dust by opposing forces and conflicting demands. While the grinding is going on, we can feel only the pain of it, and we lose all sense of any purpose or greater good that might come of it.

But try looking back at some of the painful times of your life. Can you now see any good thing that came as a result of those hard times? You may have gained a new insight into other people's needs or fears or a greater patience with their weaknesses. You may have discovered, through the very things you lack and long for, that there is something beyond your obvious wants and wishes. Your very emptiness may have guided you closer to God's heart.

Every child comes to birth through the mother's agony of labor, and Saint Paul speaks of all creation being in one huge birthing. A great deal of human suffering is unnecessary and destructive; it can and should be resisted and alleviated. Yet each person's experience of pain can sometimes be labor pain — pain that will eventually bear something good.

One of the fruits of prayer and reflection is that we learn to distinguish between the chaff and the wheat in both our negative and positive experiences. On the positive side, the chaff is the mere pleasure that may give us a temporary boost but will never satisfy our true desires, while the wheat is the joy that can never be shaken, whatever life throws at us. When it comes to our hurting, the chaff is the pain that we are called to resist and reject, because it is diminishing us, or others, as human beings. The wheat is the labor pain that is drawing us beyond ourselves, to a wholeness in God and in one another, just as it drew Jesus through Calvary into the light of the resurrection.

❧ TAKING IT FURTHER ❧

Wheat or chaff?

You might like to invite your memory and your experience to be your teachers in the art of distinguishing wheat from chaff. If you look back to past times, just notice which kinds of painful experiences have led to growth of some kind and which have left you feeling broken. This kind of reflection will help you to recognize and value the wheat and to cooperate increasingly with God's work in you.

Reflect on a "rock" time

When, in the past, have you hit the rock? Remember that time in prayer. As you look back, can you see what morsels of food and trickles of water kept you going through that time? They might have been the words or actions of a friend or stranger or some incident or encounter that changed your perspective in some way. Express, in whatever way seems right for you, your thanks to God for this healing touch.

Find yourself in the Gospels

Choose one of the Gospel narratives of Jesus' last days on earth, and read it through several times, prayerfully and peacefully. With what parts of the story or with which people do you find yourself the most emotionally engaged? What do your feelings reveal about the pain in your own life and how it connects to the suffering of Jesus? Now let your prayer move forward, when you are ready, from the agony of Friday, through the dark emptiness of Saturday, to the dawn of Sunday morning. Where has the resurrection touched your life?

19

Acting from Your Prayer

Going around in circles?

✴

To act in the Name of Jesus means to act from the
place where we are united with Jesus in love.
— HENRI NOUWEN, *BREAD FOR THE JOURNEY*

How much stillness was in *your* day today? And before you
start to feel guilty, just stop to remember what has been going on.
The demands have been coming in from all quarters, many of
them conflicting. Children, colleagues, partners, relatives, friends,
neighbors — some combination of these will have been clamor-
ing for your time and your attention in some way. The phone will
have rung, perhaps many times, or letters and bills will have arrived, asking for replies or payment or some kind of action. And
alongside all of that you will have been trying to do your normal
day-to-day tasks — cleaning, shopping, thinking what meals to
prepare, attending to birthday presents, organizing parties, keeping the home going, keeping the car running, keeping the garden
in order, to say nothing of holding your own in a paid job or
struggling through the pain and bureaucracy of being unemployed. For many people existence seems to be a relentless round
of keeping things going and unraveling life's knots. Small wonder that you feel as if you are perpetually running in circles. Small
wonder that there is no time for *you* in your day, and even less
time for God.

But I hope you are beginning to discover that God *has* been present in this endless circle in ways you may not have recognized before, that little corners of peace *can* be found in the course of this rat race. Nevertheless, coming to some kind of stillness remains one of the greatest obstacles to prayer for many people. In this chapter I suggest we pause to notice that, while the still center is an essential anchor for prayer, the busyness all around the edges also has its part to play.

Finding the Anchor Point

Coming to quietness *externally* is no big problem for most of us. We usually find it easy to still ourselves physically — perhaps because we were constantly reminded as children to sit still and stop fidgeting. But maybe that was one of the reasons we turned our activity *inwards*. Lively, exuberant children, forced to sit still, find an outlet for their suppressed energy in the racing thoughts of their minds. Why should we hope to be any different? So we face a much greater difficulty when we try to still our thoughts and minds into a receptive peacefulness. And if we do manage to come to equilibrium in our minds, to allow space for prayer, we still have to overcome our turbulent feelings and the general restlessness of our hearts.

How often do you come to the end of a day and sink exhausted into bed, thinking, *I haven't stood still all day,* or, *My feet haven't touched the ground today?* Or has anyone ever said, "I'll catch you later today" — as if you were spending your whole life running a race and even your friends have to sprint to catch up with you? Sinking those "ten feet down," when everything around you is spinning you perpetually, is a bit like dropping anchor in a stormy sea.

The time has come, perhaps, to reflect on how prayer can make it possible to be connected to a still center of ourselves, an anchor point, even while everything seems to be spinning around us. A brief excursion into an imaginative prayer picture might help to clarify things. See if it speaks to you in any way.

The Cart Wheel in the Forest

One day in prayer I let myself imagine what freedom might be like. I found myself becoming a piece of wood lying on the floor of a beautiful forest. For a while I just stayed there, enjoying the view, thinking how wonderful it felt to be free, to be myself in this lovely forest, with no interference from anyone and no tasks or duties or difficult relationships to worry about.

Then my dream of liberty was cut short. I was picked up by a pair of strong, weathered hands and examined. I felt exposed and helpless in the process. But worse was to follow. Those same strong hands took me and shaped me, planed and chiseled me into a totally new shape. I felt sore and resentful and frightened at where this unfamiliar process might be taking me.

At last the painful work was finished, and the strong hands fitted me, gently but firmly, into a wheel. One end of me was fixed to the hub, the other end to the rim. I was just a spoke in this wheel, and I didn't particularly like my neighboring spokes! What had become of my cherished freedom? As so often happens in prayer, the answer seemed to be a deafening silence! But the prayer did eventually yield its answer.

Gradually, but surely, the wheel began to *move,* and a voice somewhere inside me said: "Do you want the freedom to stay where you are, in splendid isolation on the forest floor, or do you want the freedom to move on, in the community of all my people?"

The cart wheel gathered momentum. At one end of my being I experienced the dizzy feeling of spinning through time, space, and circumstances that I could neither avoid nor significantly influence. At this outer edge — the layer of my consciousness — I spend most of my waking moments in this spinning state.

But there is another end of me, which is just as surely fixed to a still center. Prayer takes me to that still center. It connects all the holding, guiding, stabilizing power of that central hub to the spinning outer edges of my life. It holds me in real communion, whatever happens, however dizzily my life may spin. It is the heart *and* the means of my own journey and the journey of all the human family.

I think the cart wheel is a helpful picture of what it means to be the people of God. On the surface of life we are all very different, often far apart in where we live and what we do and how we see things. But we are all one at the center, that hub that is Christ. The closer we move toward that center and the more clearly we are focused on it, the closer we will move toward one another. Even those who appear to be on opposite edges of the wheel's rim will draw closer to each other as they draw closer to Christ.

But the purpose of the wheel is to *move*. And it's worth reflecting on how that movement happens. *Not* through the efforts going on at the rim, however important our striving may feel to us. Not even through the prayer that is offered at the hub. We move through the action of God, who is driving the wheel. Neither action nor contemplation is ours to achieve but God's to give.

The Potter's Wheel

I live in a town that is a center of the ceramics industry, where many people know firsthand what the potter's craft is all about. And even the rest of us, who would never manage to raise a pot from that lump of clay spinning on the table, can find a helpful picture of prayer in the potter's wheel.

In prayer we look for that kind of still and silent surrender that we could compare to the wet clay's yielding to the potter's touch. God creates us — we don't create ourselves. And when we do try to mold the world and our circumstances to our liking, we often make a mess of things. To pray is to place ourselves in God's hands and trust that God, the Potter, will form us into the people he has dreamed we shall become — that very personal representation of who God is.

But the pot needs more than the clay for its formation, and more than the Potter's skill. It needs the spinning wheel! There has to be *motion*. The spinning of my life's hours and days, that sometimes seems so senseless and frenzied to me, may be precisely that spinning that is moving me, and all creation, toward our destination in God. So often we would like nothing better than to stop the world and get off, but prayer does not allow us that kind of escape route from real life. God is shaping his dream for us, and for all creation, not only in the stillness of our hearts but in the whirling activity of our circumstances.

Contemplation in Action

The cart wheel and the potter's wheel can help us understand where our prayer is anchored and where it is active.

It is anchored in the *stillness of heart,* whenever we try to calm ourselves into a period of deliberate prayer. In this stillness we sink down below the surface storms and preoccupations of our conscious lives and open ourselves to God in hope-filled expectation, listening to whatever the Holy Spirit may bring to our inner eyes and ears.

It becomes *active* when we begin to live out what we have learned in the deep quiet of prayer. It becomes active by changing how we see things and how we react to our circumstances and by helping us make decisions in the light of gospel values. But it also becomes active by forming us (like potter's clay) into people *who make a difference* to the communities we live in — to our homes and workplaces, our neighborhoods and parishes. The prayer of each of us affects all of us. The spoke goes nowhere until it becomes part of the wheel. And the wheel will not move freely if even a single spoke is missing or broken.

Encounter at the Oasis

One Gospel woman, a Samaritan, discovered both her anchor point and her call to action in a brief encounter with Jesus. We find the story in John 4:5 – 30.

Perhaps it's a hot, dusty day in high summer. Jesus and his friends are walking through the countryside of a foreign region. They are tired and hungry and very, very thirsty. They stop beside a well that has been there for many generations. The people from the next village have to come out here every morning and every night to fetch water.

Jesus sits down on the edge of the well to rest. His friends set off to the village to buy some food for their lunch. For a few minutes he is alone there, watching his friends disappear in the hazy heat. Perhaps he wipes the sweat from his forehead and looks up. A woman with a water jar approaches the well. It isn't the proper thing for a Jewish man to do, to talk to a strange woman, especially in this foreign, hostile region. Jesus knows that, but he doesn't hesitate to draw her into conversation. Perhaps she draws closer, sits down for a rest herself, and looks into this stranger's face. They begin to talk. Jesus, she discovers, knows her better than she knows herself. Just as the ancient well has its foundations in the history of both their peoples, so Jesus takes her to the foundations of herself. They drop anchor in the silent midday heat. In Jesus she has found a still center.

But the wheel is made to move, and, when their conversation is completed, her contemplation turns into action. Verse 28 says: "The woman put down her water jar and hurried back to the town to tell the people."

And her response to all she has experienced becomes the catalyst for a mass movement. Consider verse 30: "This brought people out of the town and they made their way towards him."

We can almost see the wheels of contemplation moving into action! And we know that for us as well, this movement in our lives has its origin, its energy and guiding power, in the still place where we are anchored to the Lord in prayer.

Thinking back to the prayer of the hard place that we discussed in the previous chapter, it encourages me to reflect on this: If the Samaritan woman had had a water supply in her home, she would never have met Jesus; she would not have needed to go to the well. How often do our apparent hardships (no running water in the house) or needs lead us "outside" — to the dawn of new light and understanding?

豹 TAKING IT FURTHER 豹

Put yourself at the well

Try reading the story of the Samaritan woman in John 4:5 – 30, using the imaginative approach suggested in chapter 16. Notice your own well (wherever you personally encounter the Lord). Let yourself be there in Jesus' presence, contemplating the relationship you share. Stay for as long as you wish in that sacred place, beside the well that has its source in who you already are.

Then let Jesus send you back to your village, the place in the world where you are called to live out the consequences of your prayer. Where does this call draw you?

Have you drawn living water from your prayer? What are you going to do with that water now?

Just stop

Next time that you feel you are running in circles, let the harassment or dizziness you feel act as a trigger in your mind that says stop! Try to stand still, just for a few moments. Take a few deep breaths and imagine:

- standing with the soles of your feet flat on the ground, with deep roots going down into the earth beneath you;
- plunging your bucket down into the cool waters of a well and drawing up a draught of clear water;
- dropping anchor in the middle of a gale and letting your life's boat come to stillness and security.

These moments of recollection will pass, but you will have tapped into the true source of your energy, and you will be empowered *to move on*, because:

- your feet are made for walking;
- the water is for carrying back to the village;
- the boat is built to sail.

20

Approaching Contemplative Prayer

From words into silence

Through contemplation you become a fountain that pours forth living water in all directions. Anyone who comes within the radius of that fountain — old or young, rich or poor, man or woman, saint or sinner, friend or enemy — gets splashed by love.
— WILLIAM JOHNSTONE, *BEING IN LOVE*

At the beginning of this exploration of prayer, we looked at ways of praying with one's own life's story; we used the image of the river as a way to describe the flow of life so far, with its joys and its difficulties. Today I would like to invite you to reflect on another river that helps me to move closer to that simple loving awareness of the presence of God that we call "contemplation."

Called into the Depths of God

This is the river described by the prophet Ezekiel, in his vision of his own relationship with God. Ezekiel 47:1 – 12 describes a spring of fresh water gurgling up under the doorway to the temple. You might imagine the temple to be your own life, or your own inner-most being, your heart, where God dwells. And the spring bubbles up as an expression from within you of your desire to be in a loving relationship with God and to express this relationship in prayer.

But the search for prayer is not always straightforward. See what happens to Ezekiel. He comes out of the temple by the north gate and is led all around the building, counterclockwise, until he gets to the east gate and discovers the stream of prayer. If he'd only known, he could have had an easier journey. He could have at least walked clockwise and cut out three quarters of the circular journey round the temple! (We can all be wise with hindsight.)

However convoluted and long-winding the path, let's assume that we have arrived at that east gate and found that trickle of a stream that is flowing there — flowing out in the direction of the dawn. Only a trickle, but full of hope and desire. We might follow it as it flows out into the unknown country, meaning the rest of our lives.

Ezekiel notices how his stream is deepening. How do you feel about your stream? If we were in Ezekiel's situation, if we were to wander five hundred yards downstream and test the waters, we would find ourselves still only ankle-deep. Prayer is happening perhaps, but it is lapping around our ankles and not making much difference yet to the way we live. Another five hundred yards, and we are already knee-deep. Prayer is beginning to challenge us and become a force to be reckoned with. Yet another five hundred yards on, we find ourselves waist-high in the water. Living with prayer is demanding a great deal from us, but God is also showing us his increasing trust in us and sharing more and more of himself with us — for, after all, *he is the stream* that is flowing through our hearts and bringing us to the fullness of life.

Finally, when we have come the last five hundred yards downstream, the trickle of prayer that we barely noticed at the beginning has become a river so wide and deep that we can no longer cross it. We can only surrender ourselves totally to its power and let it carry us onward in faith to the sea of perfect communion with God and all his children, which is our heart's destination. Will we ever dare take that kind of risk? Notice what happens at this point in our prayer. So far we have been measuring the river and noticing its increasing depth. In our prayer we tend to do this — gauge how well we are doing or how far we have come. But in truth, a loving relationship cannot be weighed and measured nor can one person's unique love for God or another person ever be compared with any other. When the river becomes too deep for our paddling and our wading, *then the focus changes.*

From now on in Ezekiel's story, the focus is on the river, rather than on the person who is experiencing it. In our parallel prayer metaphor, see what happens as a result: When we turn our focus away from ourselves and our achievements and toward the river itself, we notice the surroundings — trees growing alongside it, their roots watered by its flow, their branches bearing fruit in every season to feed God's hungry people. We see the plants and medicinal herbs along the riverbank, watered by its flow to bring healing to a broken world. We see fishermen dangling their poles in its waters and drawing good catches of fish, to nourish their families. The more the river widens and deepens, the more abundant the life it sustains, until the whole of creation is brought to fruitfulness and the dry desert places burst into blossom.

I believe Ezekiel's vision is more than a poetic prophecy for the coming of God's reign in his world. I believe it is a picture of what prayer can become for *every* person. I believe it because, again and again, I have seen people's struggle to find the east gate and discover that tiny trickle — the first springing up of a desire to pray. And I have seen their disbelief, wonder, and joy, as their little trickle has deepened and widened. I have seen them challenged by their prayer and by the joys and the pain that a personal relationship with God brings. And I have seen them at the point where their focus has shifted from themselves to the desert plains through which the river of grace is flowing, and they have realized that prayer *is* that flow of grace, and that they themselves have become part of it.

Called into Transformation

A few weeks ago I spent a day on the west coast of Wales, visiting friends. We went for a long walk along the beach and among the sand dunes. We had the gift of time that day. Nothing was rushing us. We could linger for as long as we wished and really see and experience the life of the shoreline.

This oasis in the midst of life's busyness also happened to come at a time when a close friend had just been tragically bereaved. Untimely death was very much on our minds — as well as large, unanswered questions about the apparently senseless extinguishing of a young woman's life. Perhaps you can imagine our thoughts and our mood as we walked along the shore.

And perhaps for us, as for the first disciples who met the risen Lord on the shores of Galilee (John 21:1–14), there was a stranger on the shore, waiting to greet us, to invite us to share a barbecue breakfast and to point our hearts to the side of our lives where the net-breaking catch of fish would be found so unexpectedly. Now, as I look back and reflect on that walk with friends, I can certainly see ways in which God made his presence known to us that day. And I would like to relate to you just one part of that walk, because for me it was a picture of, and an invitation into, the kind of prayer that is transforming.

We saw our first prayer clue in the carpet of flowers that blanketed the grassy dunes — pink sea thrift and golden vetches, delicate lemon and purple violets, and tiny blue germander speedwells. Among them fluttered a host of perfect black and crimson butterflies. We walked on, treading carefully, and our daughter stopped, as she had so often done as a little girl, to gaze at the wealth of little black and green tufted caterpillars crawling in the grass. It was hard to imagine that these little creatures would also soon be flying with black and crimson wings. We knew about the transformation that awaited them. We knew the biology of it, but we had no felt experience of the miracle.

We sat down among the dunes to enjoy our picnic lunch, and suddenly we noticed what looked like dried-up seedpods or half-dead leaves clinging to some of the grass stalks. My friend pointed out that these were actually the pupae of the tiny butterflies we had seen. When I realized what she was saying, I looked at the little yellow seedpods in a very different light. Inside that still and silent pod an amazing act of transformation was taking place.

I was so thrilled by this discovery that, when I returned home, I looked up the life cycle of butterflies. I read that the evolving caterpillar spins a thread from its own body to attach itself firmly to the stalk of a plant; this thread will hold it throughout the pupa stage. It seems to me that we do something like this when we allow God to draw us into what is often called contemplative prayer. All that we can do, in such prayer, is to cling to God by our own longings and to trust him to hold us. What happens then seems similar to the experience of the chrysalis. Of course we can't imagine what it is like to be a chrysalis, but at least we can surmise that this is a completely *passive* state. The busy caterpillar, whose daily task was to find food and to grow, now allows itself merely to hang, quite still and silent, apparently doing nothing and looking like a lifeless seedpod.

But seedpods are far from lifeless! They actually contain all the plant's tomorrows, just as wondrously as the ovaries of an unborn female child contain all the eggs that may ever become new life in the adult woman. And perhaps contemplative prayer is like that. It looks and feels like nothing. In the depths of contemplation there is no active imagination at work, no thinking, no feeling, no image, no petition or intercession. What there *is,* is that slender line of connection, linking us to the God who holds us. And there is God, nothing but God, or as they say where I come from, "Nobbut God."

A lovely and familiar picture of contemplative prayer is often explained by the story of a French peasant who went into his parish church every day, without fail, for a period of quiet. He would simply sit at the back of the church and gaze into the air. The parish priest noticed this, and one day he asked the man about his church visits and what he was actually doing. His answer: "I just look at God. And he looks at me. And we are content."

It seems like nothing at all — perhaps the same kind of nothingness that was happening as Jesus hung dying on the cross, like a pupa hanging by a thread to a stalk. But the butterfly book gave me one more piece of vital information. The pupa skin, it said, has holes in it, so that the evolving chrysalis can get oxygen, because, in fact, a great deal of energy is being expended there inside the

172 / Using the Word as Our Guide

pupa skin. It is the *energy of transformation*. That inert, dormant creature, hanging passively on a stalk, is, even as we gaze, being transformed from a hairy, greedy caterpillar into a beautiful, life-renewing butterfly.

If you didn't know about butterflies, there is no way that you could possibly guess what miracle is happening in the silent darkness of the pupa. And the same is true of the passive silence of deep contemplative prayer. Only God knows about our butterflies. *We* still live in the realm of the caterpillar, who thinks that life is about activity and survival. But, in contemplative prayer, we are drawn beyond our caterpillar selves, trusting that the nothingness is leading to everything, trusting in the butterfly that is still far beyond our imagination.

How Do We Begin?

Probably most of us, if we think of contemplative prayer at all, regard it as something that is beyond us and practiced only by a few contemplative monks and nuns whose whole lives are devoted to prayer. Yet I have heard respected and experienced spiritual guides say that contemplation is often given to those you would least expect—to harassed mothers and people who think they can't pray, to children, to the sick and dying, to people with no head learning about prayer or Scripture or theology. God sometimes seems to speak, heart to heart, in this mysterious way, to the untaught and unpracticed. None of us should imagine that the ways of contemplative prayer are closed to us, because God is always infinitely larger than our expectations.

I suggest that creation itself gives us a gateway. In every moment of our lives, a silent, invisible miracle of exchange is taking place. We breathe out the air that our bodies no longer need, which is mainly carbon dioxide, a waste product for us but the very thing that the green leaves on the trees and plants need to produce their own energy. So they receive our carbon dioxide and, through the process of photosynthesis, produce not only their own life energy, but also oxygen—a waste product for them, but the very thing *we* need to live. Whenever I stop my busyness for a few moments to look around me, I am amazed at this arrangement, and it makes me think of prayer.

So perhaps a good way to open our hearts up to the gift of contemplation is simply to become still, and, quite literally, to breathe *out* our waste—all that clogs us and deadens us—and to breathe *in* God's renewing life, as we breathe in the fresh oxygen that the plants have made for us. This simple, deliberate breathing exercise can become something like what the French peasant was doing as he looked at God and God looked at him. We are becoming aware of the mysterious exchange of life between ourselves and God. And there is no reason that any period of quiet might not become prayer of this kind.

There may be other creatures who can help you cross the threshold of contemplation. If there is a baby in the family, try simply holding her in your arms as she sleeps and letting God hold both of you in his. Nothing more. No deep thoughts. No search for meaning. Just be there.

A cat (if you are not allergic to them!) can also be a great aid to prayer. My own cat loves to sleep round my neck. At first I found this disturbing, but when he has settled into a particular hollow (perhaps where he can feel my pulse), he will lie there, quite still, just purring deeply, until he falls asleep and the purring ceases. When he does this, I let myself find a hollow close to God's pulse, and let my own prayer become just a sleepy purr and then the silence of content. Or you might discover prayer on a park bench. The other day I was in Hyde Park, and I spent a few minutes listening to the deep-throated cooing of the pigeons. I wanted to join them, because, in their way, they were engaged in contemplative prayer, simply expressing, in this peaceful murmur, the song of their beings.

In your own home, prayer awaits you in the opening of a flower, the rising of your bread dough, or the steady, imperceptible development of a child. Spend time in silence, aware of the wonder that is being unfolded in your cakes and your children, your houseplants or your garden. For this is the essence of contemplative prayer — simple *awareness,* allowing God to be God, without trying to put the limitations of shape or meaning around him.

Contemplation, like all prayer, is pure gift, and not anything we can achieve. It happens when prayer becomes, wholly and utterly, the flow of God's grace, transforming the land it flows through, like Ezekiel's stream. Or it happens when we lose consciousness of our own part in it and become simply receptors and carriers of grace. It happens when we realize that our transformation depends on nothing but God's grace and love, and, like the chrysalis, let go of all activity to try to achieve our own redemption.

When we try to describe it, we fail, for it lies beyond the world of words. We can open our hearts to it by the practice of awareness, but we cannot bring it about, any more than we can force a flower to open or an egg to hatch. And in our silent, trustful waiting, we are acknowledging that God is God, the source and the destination, the means and the end of all our prayer, whatever form it may take.

❧ TAKING IT FURTHER ❧

A baby's gaze

No words can lead you into wordlessness, but you might like to spend some time just gazing at a baby's face — perhaps a baby in your family or a small child you notice. Watch as the baby gazes at some object. She is seeing that object for the very first time, and her eyes are wide with wonder and delight. Let her touch you with her awareness. She is seeing creation with God's eyes. She is actually in deep and joyous contemplation. She is in prayer. And probably she will never again pray with such effortless intensity.

But there will be moments in her life when this first profound awareness of the mystery of things will return. Perhaps when she falls in love. When she holds her own child in her arms. When she is transported by some moment of joy so fleeting, yet so solid that she knows she is in touch with her own deepest reality. We all know such moments, and we have explored something of their meaning in the pages of this book.

Must we wait until these moments visit us, like passing butterflies? I remember once, at the start of a retreat, being invited by my guide to spend a few hours walking around, with my eyes open, until something in the world around me caught my attention, and then just to remain, "quietly present to that presence." You might try this exercise for yourself, asking for the grace to see with God's eyes—or with Adam's eyes—some small part of creation as if for the very first time and with the very first human eyes. Then respond to God in silence and in wonder.

PART FOUR

Stumbling Blocks and Stepping Stones

Two of the most commonly experienced problems in prayer are explored in this last part: distraction and the vexed question of whether God really answers prayer. Some helps for prayer are also introduced: the gift of companionship in prayer, whether individual or in community; suggestions for keeping a spiritual journal; and the grace that awaits us if we look beyond our boundaries.

Finally, was Saint Paul really serious when he urged us to "pray constantly" (1 Thessalonians 5:17)? Decide for yourself whether prayer can become a way of life so natural that it informs every moment of your being.

21

Learning to Focus

Distractions, detours, destinations

✳

The surface of a fast-flowing river is often broken by
waves and eddies in which the water seems to rush off
in all directions and even contrary to the main flow;
while underneath all this busyness there is a constant,
steady current which can be felt more strongly below
the surface where the river is deepest.
— David Lonsdale, *Eyes to See, Ears to Hear*

However incompetent we may feel in the art of praying, we can consider ourselves experts when it comes to distractions. The question pops up over and over again: How can I stay with prayer and free myself of the endless stream of distractions?

Perhaps you remember the image of the stormy sea used in an earlier chapter. Not far below the storm is, in fact, peaceful water. But what is happening on the surface *seems* much more real and insistent than what is happening deep down. Now that we have looked at the possibility of a deep contemplative prayer — prayer that is active in us while we think nothing is going on at all — it becomes easier to see that our distractions in prayer are operating on the surface, and this is why they seem to dominate us so much and claim our attention so insistently.

There is no cast-iron solution to the problem of distractions in prayer. If there were, someone would surely have patented it by now, and we would all be standing in line to buy it. But a couple of general guidelines may be helpful.

Ignore the Attention Seekers

When distractions come, remember that they are only bobbing on the surface of your prayer, and they do not have the power to deflect you from your course unless you choose to *give* them that power.

You might compare it with driving a car. As you drive, you are thinking continually about your destination and how much you are looking forward to arriving. During the course of the journey, all kinds of things may happen. It may begin to rain, and you have to fiddle with the windshield wipers. The radio program may start to bore you, so you turn to another station. The children may be squabbling in the backseat. The road may be blocked, and you may have to follow a detour. Or the tire may blow, and you have to change it.

All these things can be incredibly annoying; they can waste your time and set you on edge, but in the evening, when you are relaxing at your destination, you hardly remember them. I think prayer distractions are like that, and they should not be given more importance than they deserve. Instead of attending to them, focus on the ten-feet-down approach. Acknowledge the disturbance, but keep returning to your deeper sense of the destination, which is to be close to God and your own center.

But Look after the Genuine Calls

Some of the apparently trivial distractions in prayer are worth dealing with when they arise, because they won't go away. These are things such as, *Did I turn the gas off? Is the baby safe?* Such matters are easy to deal with and they *must* be dealt with, because you will certainly not come to inner peace until you have resolved them. Sometimes the phone rings during my prayer, and, because I have no idea whether the call is important or not, I answer it. So I just apologize to God, as to a friend, and ask God to excuse me for a minute. Then I let the issue go and come back to prayer when I can, without any unnecessary agonizing, which would be another distraction!

A friend once gave me two very helpful and encouraging pieces of advice about distractions. She reminded me that, though I feel as if I have been distracted fifty times in half an hour of prayer, it is equally true that I have also turned back to God fifty times as well, and such a conversion record is no bad thing.

Her other piece of wisdom was borrowed from Luther, who said: "Distractions are like birds flying round your head. You can't stop them flying, but you don't have to let them build nests in your hair." This is really saying that if you keep your eyes on the road, then the swipe of the windshield wipers won't have the power to make you go off course.

To this I would just add one piece of advice: *Distractions are not sins.* They are not a matter for confession. The guilt they generate is a false guilt and a further distraction. Don't let it tie you in knots.

When Is a Distraction Not a Distraction?

Sometimes, however, our distractions can be trying to tell us something. If a particular distraction just won't let you go, try asking God to show you its significance. In effect, you are taking your distraction into prayer; when you do this the distraction may actually become part of the destination, because it originates in something that needs your prayerful attention.

A friend once told me of his experience, trying to pray in a quiet chapel in a retreat house. His employer was laying people off, and he was justifiably anxious about his future. He had come to the retreat house in the hope of putting these anxieties aside for a while. As he sat quietly praying in the chapel, a cleaning lady arrived with her vacuum cleaner. She worked her way noisily around the chapel, and my friend found himself becoming more and more frustrated. Eventually she unplugged the machine and started to leave. The man breathed a sigh of relief and looked forward to the return of silence. But just before the cleaning lady left, she came up alongside him and tapped his shoulder. He started at the unexpected interruption, and then she said, "Can you turn the lights out, love, when you go?"

My friend chose to smile at the way the woman's words had bounced into his attempts at prayer. Then the distraction of her presence turned into an internal distraction: He suddenly remembered a poster hanging on the wall at the office: "Will the last person to leave please turn out the lights?" It was someone's attempt at making a joke about the layoffs. Being reminded of that bit of ironic humor brought the whole issue of downsizing, which he had been suppressing, to the forefront of his heart and mind. He was able to bring it honestly to God in his prayer, and during the evening he felt able to discuss it with others and find new ways to deal with his anxieties.

This experience showed him and me that we shouldn't throw distractions away too readily. We may be throwing good prayer out along with them.

"There's an Overturned Semi on Route . . ."

Hearing these words from the car radio can raise the hairs on the back of your neck! In our family this usually means a quick rummage for the road map, impatient admonitions to half-asleep passengers to search for a suitable detour, and a foul mood over it all.

I recall a trip we once made across northern Europe along the German autobahn system. A tedious journey at the best of times, but that day the standing traffic tailed back for miles. Fortunately, salvation was at hand. A system of detours was also in place, and we slipped off at the next exit, followed the detour, arrived back on the autobahn, having bypassed the obstruction.

I noticed that while we were driving along the detour, we lost all sense of the real journey. Suddenly we were not on a clear, straight road anymore but winding our way through towns and villages that we never planned to visit! In such a situation we can easily become preoccupied with these unexpected "minor visions," which may either delight us or depress us. And if we had stopped to take our bearings at most any point, we might have calculated that we were traveling in the wrong direction. Then it would have been all too easy to panic. From this trivial incident, I drew some conclusions about distractions:

- While you are taking a detour, you lose sight, temporarily, of your destination.

- The detour diverts your energy away from the real journey. On the highway this energy is measured in gallons of fuel. On our inner journey it is our vital spiritual energy.

- But if you follow the detour signs, you will eventually arrive back on the right road.

The Power of a Piece of Thread

What form might these detours take in our prayer? I tend to see them as a kind of Ariadne's thread. Ariadne, of classical mythology, helped Theseus find his way out of the Labyrinth by giving him a ball of string with which he could retrace his steps. The German detour numbers on the side roads are exactly like that. They provide a ball of string to bring you back to where you want to be. When I lose myself in distractions and detours in prayer, I often find that a marker like this can help me get back. I might, for example, need to reread the Scripture passage with which I started the prayer. Or I might hold a particular phrase or mantra in my mind. When you are on the detour, there are no signs to your real destination. The only guide you have are the detour signs or numbers themselves and your knowledge of the overall map. On your inner journey, the only compass you can trust is your own desire for the ultimate destination. Through all distractions, your need for prayer and your desire for God can bring you back again and again.

After World War II, thousands of people in Europe were displaced and became refugees trekking across the continent. One such person was Hanna, a twelve-year-old schoolgirl. When hostile troops moved into her home town in Silesia, now part of Poland, she and her family became homeless. Her mother remained behind with the youngest child, a two-year-old. Her father and brother managed to stay together but were interned in a refugee camp. Hanna, alone and with nothing, started to walk. All she had was an address of a relative hundreds of miles away in the far west of Germany. She walked. And she walked. And somehow or other she kept on walking, week after week, month after month, until she finally arrived. What kept her walking? No doubt there were plenty of distractions — threats to her safety or temptations to give up and let herself fall into despair. What kept her going was that address in her pocket of the place, far away, where she would be welcomed and received. There was no energy to visit all the attractions on the way. She needed every ounce of energy just to keep going.

And so do we! We need to keep our fingers curled around that address in our pockets that reminds us every passing moment that our destination is with God and that this is where our whole desire is focused, however interesting the detours may become.

Yet, as in the physical situation of a blocked road, sometimes it is necessary to make a detour. Perhaps much of our experience of feeling lost and distracted is just this — our energies are being deflected because we have to get past an obstruction. But God's guiding is so much like the German detour systems; if I follow the right detour number — my inner compass or my Ariadne's thread — it *will* bring me back to the straight road, after the obstruction has been circumvented.

Moving, swiftly, from classical mythology to modern technology, I must report that while I have been writing this chapter, I have been distracted:

- By a huge thud that could have been something serious. It had to be investigated, and it turned out to be a pigeon that flew into the upstairs window.

- By a letter that required me to reply and send off a parcel before the post office closed.

- By a failure of my e-mail system that forced me to make an urgent phone call to get it back on line so that I could receive a message I need for a meeting tomorrow.

Yet the focus of my morning has remained on the task of writing this chapter. This is my Ariadne's thread: The page I am working on has stayed faithfully on my computer screen, and the little black cursor has even stayed at the word where I left off. And the desire that keeps me going — and keeps me coming back! — is the overriding desire to get these thoughts down for my readers, and this has the power to attract me more even than the poor pigeon or the e-mail system's indigestion. I don't feel guilty because I have stopped to attend these other things. They had to be done. And I don't even feel unduly frustrated, because my firm intention to write this chapter has not been permanently undermined by these diversions.

I feel that my prayer is like that too. My heart's focus on God remains, like that page on the screen, even if my mind and body are at the back door, burying the pigeon. And my attentiveness never leaves the point where my heart is parked. And my desire for communion with God in prayer is, in the end, strong enough to keep me coming back.

The Toy Magnet Challenges
Isaac Newton

In case you are still worried about the power your distractions seem to have to divert your attention and destroy the focus of your prayer, try thinking of your heart's desire for God in terms of an iron filing being drawn steadily and reliably to a vast magnet that we might call the heart of God. This is as sure and certain as the fact that we are held on planet Earth by the power of gravity. We don't spend time worrying that gravity might fail and we might consequently float off into space. As far as our understanding can tell, there is absolutely no danger of the laws of gravity breaking down. It is equally certain (so we say with our lips) that the love of God holds us in a way that will never let us go, whatever we do or fail to do.

But you can override the laws of gravity with a pocket magnet that any child can buy for a dollar. You can pick up a pin from the floor and force it *temporarily* to defy gravity. This thought used to depress me. I could see in it the potential in my distractions and addictions to pull me off course and draw me away from God. Until I realized one morning that the pocket magnet, together with everything it can attract to itself, is itself held to earth by the law of gravity.

In the same way, I believe, all the things that have the power to distract us are likewise held in the magnetic field of God, who is infinitely larger than all the distractions that ever were, are, or shall be.

Likewise, the ocean of God "in whom we live, and move, and have our being" (Acts 17:28 KJV) is deeper and more vast than the passing disturbance that makes waves on the surface of our consciousness. On this we can depend.

❈ TAKING IT FURTHER ❈

Draw your life

A colleague of mine, who taught children to play violin, once told me that the worst thing you can do when you are trying to teach a child is to tell her to "concentrate!" As soon as she begins to "concentrate," she is concentrating on the art of concentration and no longer on the art of playing the violin. It made good sense to me, and not just in the field of music!

So the worst thing I could suggest, by way of an exercise, is anything that focuses your attention on your distractions. The only thing that helps us deal with distractions is to focus on the *destination* and to ignore the distractions as far as is humanly possible. A more sensible exercise might be simply: Now forget this chapter and move on!

However, there is something that can help us see our distractions in perspective, and that, ironically, is to magnify them and make them life-size.

To do this, try drawing a little sketch of the path your life has taken so far. Notice its main direction. Where have your desires, dreams, and energies been invested primarily? How might you describe your desired destination in this journey? Let this become the main road in your picture.

Now notice the various side tracks you have taken. What were they about? Where did they lead you? Did you go down those tracks to circumvent some perceived obstruction or difficulty in your life? Are there any cul-de-sacs along the way? Did you get stuck in them, or did you find your way out? How do you feel now about the shape of your journey? Whatever convolutions it displays, it has nevertheless brought you to where you are today. How does that make you feel?

If any of these questions particularly draws your attention, stay with it and let it help you understand better the power of distractions as compared with the power that pulls you forward on the real journey.

God and chaos

When your mind and thoughts are all over the place and you feel, as John Milton once wrote, that chaos is come again, call to mind what God did with the first primeval chaos (Genesis 1:1–2). Ask God to let God's Spirit hover over your personal chaos. Surrender the task of creation back into God's hands.

This may not immediately reveal a solution, but it will draw your heart down toward its center in God, leaving your troubled distraction up on the surface where the storm will blow itself out in its own time. It will take you to the place of calm where you will be able to see the real issues involved.

Can you remember?

Yesterday, last week, last month, you struggled with a bout of distraction in your prayer. (If this isn't true for you, it certainly is for me!) Can you remember what that distraction was about? What does that tell you about the permanence of its power over you?

22

Looking for God
When God Is Silent

Does God answer prayer?

✳

I sent a sigh to seek thee out,
Deep drawn in pain,
Wing'd like an arrow: but my scout
Returns in vain
— GEORGE HERBERT, "THE SEARCH"

Does God really hear our prayer? This difficult question confronts all of us from time to time. Why doesn't God (apparently) keep his promise to give us all we ask, if we only believe? Many a fervent Christian's faith has been tested when heartfelt prayer, to make a sick person well, for instance, has not been answered in any way that we can recognize.

Maybe the pictures of the cart wheel and the potter's wheel from chapter 19 can help you move a little closer to that mystery surrounding the way God does or (more often) does not appear to answer prayer. I invite you to let these wheels adjust your focus a little.

Think of the wheel as it spins; the hub of the activity is at the center. Our whole universe spins around an invisible center of gravity, just as the cart wheel turns about its hub and the potter's wheel spins around its spindle. The rim of the cart wheel, just as the clay on the potter's wheel, can see only the view from the edge. It takes the driver of the cart to know where the wheels are moving to. The pot needs the potter's eyes to know what all the motion is leading to. We are living, consciously, all the time on that outer edge of God's creating, redeeming work in creation. It should not surprise us that we can't very often see what God is about!

We who are parents often have to deny our children the little things they ask for so as to give them what they need and what will draw them forward to a fuller, healthier life. If God seems deaf to you, try adjusting your focus away from the little bit of reality you can see from your position on the edge of all the motion and commotion, and remind yourself that you are in the hands of the One who alone can see creation in its entirety.

A Human Gateway to God

A friend recently lent me a video of *The Robe,* which tells a story of how Jesus' seamless robe, gambled away by the soldiers at Jesus' crucifixion, might have gone on to affect its owner in powerful and disturbing ways, until that owner was eventually drawn into a new faith.

One moving scene in this film is of the Robe owner meeting Miriam, a crippled woman in the village of Cana. Miriam had been a young girl at the time of Jesus' first miracle, at a wedding in Cana. She alone, of all the villagers, had not attended this wedding because it was too painful for her to face the fact that because of her physical limitations she would never be a bride herself. As the villagers left her that day to go to the wedding, she had been enclosed in her own bitterness and pain. When they returned, they found her singing. No less physically crippled than before, she had nevertheless been miraculously healed. Her crippled heart had been made whole.

When Marcellus, the Roman tribune who owned the Robe, challenged Miriam with the taunt that Jesus had not, after all, answered her prayer and cured her body, she admitted that this same thought had troubled her for years. Surely the Lord who had freed her heart could have given her back the use of her body? But in time she had become aware of a great gift concealed in her handicapped life. Had she been physically healed, she would have been just a special case, a miracle story perhaps, but not a woman with whom other women could identify. Remaining disabled, she had become a gateway to God for other people with handicaps — a living testimony that it is possible to live a full life even when physically limited.

The Robe is fiction. But perhaps you know someone like Miriam. Someone whom God seems unwilling to cure, but who has become a special messenger of God's grace in ways that would not have been possible otherwise. A wounded healer. Perhaps you are such a person yourself. Perhaps, amid all the confusion of your unanswered prayers, your life is communicating the gospel so that it resonates in other people's lives in ways you may never be aware of.

I have a friend who is blind and his life has been wounded in many other ways, through the blows of history, war, persecution, and family breakup. He finds his blindness very hard to bear. The situation seems to defy faith and the heartrending "Why, Lord, *why?*" of prayer. God could have cured him, surely. But if God had cured my friend's blindness, countless classes of small children in a local school for the blind would never have had the healing experience of sitting around him in their classrooms, week by week, year by year, listening to his stories, hearing his gentle, confidence-inspiring voice, learning from him about blindness *from the inside*. These children have learned to trust him, and, through him, to trust themselves in a dangerous world. And we, his sighted friends, have learned from him that insight (which he has in abundance) is an even more precious gift than sight. And so a deeper purpose has been fulfilled than our partial prayers could ever have formulated.

A Wand or a Spear?

I get very frustrated when Christian churches seemingly seduce people into expecting the wave of a divine magic wand to answer their prayers and fulfill their desires. This is the opposite of how things work. The good news is not that God will fix us with his wand but that, when life fixes us with its spear, that spear will open up a flow of grace within us. If the wand existed, it might satisfy the lesser wants and wishes with which we sometimes bombard God in our prayers, but the spear is the way to the deeper, more enduring issues of our lives. It was a spear, after all, that pierced Jesus' side on Calvary. From that wound flowed grace for all of us. I believe that grace flows also from our own wounds, our broken hearts and lives.

When the puzzle is complete, I believe *we will find that God has been answering the prayers we have not yet found the words to express.* We will discover that God has all along been fulfilling the truest desires of our hearts that we do not acknowledge, because they lie buried under layers of lesser wants and wishes. Perhaps our simplest and most sincere prayer might be that God will open our eyes to become increasingly aware of our deeper desires, which he is continually seeking to fulfill. Perhaps it isn't so much that God is deaf, as that we ourselves are still blind to what we truly long for.

Missing the Obvious

Writers never see the mistakes in their own manuscripts; manuscripts always have to be proofread by someone unfamiliar with the text, who will read what is actually there and not what he expects to be there. The writer will invariably see what she *intended* to write. The proofreader will read what was actually written. And it is amazing just how many mistakes a proofreader will pick up, even though the writer was sure that she had checked and double-checked it.

Perhaps prayer is like that. We don't see God's answers to our prayers, because our minds are completely tuned in to what we *expect* God to do, or even what we, in our wisdom, have *instructed* him to do. And our own expectation represents a very small part when set against the whole cosmic range of God's possibilities. Thus it becomes easy to miss the obvious, because we are waiting for events to unfold as we had planned them, and we are blind to the ways in which God *is active* in the situation.

This blindness can be exacerbated even more if we don't really *want* any solution to the problem other than the one we have worked out for ourselves. I remember once giving God very detailed instructions about how to solve a particular problem. I had worked it all out for him. All God needed to do was put his signature to it and get on with it. Imagine my chagrin when he delivered a completely different solution, which I could never, in my wildest dreams, have thought up, and one that caused me considerable personal discomfort!

To move beyond this kind of habitual blockage, try turning your prayer on its head. Instead of focusing on what you are asking God to do in your life and then waiting to see if he does it, try noticing what God is *actually* doing in your life and reflecting on how that is revealing his unceasing engagement with your deepest desires.

As so often in prayer, the key is in the focus. Either we don't *see* God's answers, or we don't *want* God's answers. Often we fail to see God's answers to our prayers, because our focus is on our own expectations rather than on God's limitless power to move our hearts closer to their own fulfillment. And, if we are praying for others but don't want any answers that we haven't invented ourselves, the focus is surely on ourselves and on the satisfaction of our pride in doing good and not on the real needs and desires of the person we are praying for.

We might experience a radically different perspective on things if we could ask instead: "What is God doing right now, in my daily life (or in the life of the person I am praying for)?"

If we can trust God to be doing what best fulfills our true desires — for ourselves and for those we pray for — then we may see answers to prayers that we had never dared to hope for.

An Inside Job?

In chapter 9 we looked at the possibility that God might answer our prayers for others by challenging us to become the answers to them ourselves. As I see it, part of the power of prayer is to awaken our own hearts (not God's!) to what lies at the root of our desires

or the core of our needs. This awakening concerning any particular issue or concern may be a signal to turn the dreaming into
action. When making any prayer, perhaps we should assume that
we ourselves are on the short list of candidates for answering it in
practical ways.

A prayer for success on an exam, for example, is not likely to be
answered unless we invest some effort ourselves. That much is
obvious. But what about prayer for issues of social justice? We may
beg God to convert the hearts and minds of our leaders, but what
choices do we make in practice—when we vote or come up against
unfair or unjust behavior on our doorstep or in our own families?

Here are a few questions we may need to ask ourselves, when
we reflect on our prayer:

- In what practical ways might *I* begin to answer this prayer?

- Do I really want this prayer to be answered, and am I willing
  to leave the form of the answer entirely to God?

- How much am I prepared to pay (in money, time, energy, patience, good will) to bring about an answer to this prayer? This
  doesn't mean that I bribe God to do things my way, but it does
  mean that I count and willingly commit to the cost in personal
  terms of cooperating with God on the issue I'm praying about.

That We Might See . . .

In Luke 18:35–43 and 19:1–10, two stories are told side by side,
each about a person who wanted to see.

The first, a blind beggar on the roadside near Jericho, heard a
crowd going past and asked what all the fuss was about. When
told that Jesus was passing by, the beggar called out to Jesus for
help, but the crowd tried to silence him. Undeterred, he shouted
all the louder. Jesus heard the cries, stopped, and asked the man,
"What do you want me to do for you?" *Lord, that I might see!*
He begged, "Let me see again" (verse 41). And the man's sight was
restored. We are told that he then followed Jesus, praising God,

and that all who saw the effects of the miracle were similarly drawn to praise God.

The second person, Zacchaeus, had a different kind of blindness. He was too short to see over the heads of the crowd. Desperate to catch a glimpse of Jesus, he climbed a tree to gain a better view. That might have been the end of the matter, but Jesus noticed Zacchaeus up the tree and stopped at that very spot, peered up at him, and called him into something far beyond what he had hoped for — or felt himself ready for. Luke 19:5 says: "Zacchaeus, come down. Hurry, because I am to stay at your house today." This turn of events caused an outbreak of complaint in the crowd. Zacchaeus was a notorious sinner, a senior tax official who had lined his pockets with their money. Perhaps he regretted the sudden sweep of the searchlight that his perch in the tree had brought upon him. The price of seeing was being seen. There, in the presence of the burning integrity of the Lord, Zacchaeus had no choice but to acknowledge the truth about himself. It was his conversion experience. The story ends with Jesus' words of loving, healing acceptance: "This man too is a son of Abraham" (verse 9). It was the turn of the crowd, now, to see. It was no longer possible simply to demonize those parts of God's creation that they did not like. Like Zacchaeus, they had come out to see the Lord; like Zacchaeus, they went home having been challenged to see themselves.

I think that these two stories can give us insight into the nature of our prayer and how God might answer it.

• Nothing clarifies our minds so much as raw need. The blind beggar knew exactly what he wanted. He focused his whole attention on the one thing he knew would change his life. Prayer that comes from such need seems to bring us straight to the heart of God. When we bring our needs to God, are we not begging him for that one thing that will change our lives? And will we recognize it when it is given? Will we trust God's judgment, or our own, as to what that one thing really is?

• What effort are we willing to make to open ourselves up to God's answers? The blind beggar had to overcome the hostility of the crowd and keep on persisting until he caught the Lord's ear. How do we score on the persistence scale? Zacchaeus made the effort to climb a tree. How far will we go to meet the Lord?

• The answer to prayer can sometimes turn the prayer on its head. We ask to see, and we find ourselves being seen. Prayer turns out to be a blank check. Are we really willing to sign that check and hand it over, unconditionally, to the Lord?

• Prayer may be solitary and individual, but the answer affects the whole community. Everyone was caught up in praise following the healing of the blind beggar. When Zacchaeus made his bid to see, the searchlight of truth fell on everyone. God's action in the life of any of us is action in the life of all God's creation. We are affected by the answers to one another's prayers. Are our prayers just about "me" (perhaps at the expense of others), or are they about the needs of all God's family? If God responds to the desires I have in my own little world, how will this response affect those around me? No caring parent would give one child in the family something that would harm or deprive the other siblings.

Perhaps, then, instead of bombarding God with requests for what is not, we might try, instead, asking God to open our eyes to see what *is*.

❧ TAKING IT FURTHER ❧

To be that kind of brother

The other day I heard a story in a homily. The preacher said he had heard it on the radio and believed it to be a true story of a man's conversion experience.

A rich business tycoon was driving through a poor part of town in his new Cadillac. He parked it to attend to some business, and when he came back, a street kid was peering in the windows. Thinking the boy was up to no good, the businessman challenged him, but the boy just gazed at him, with awe-filled eyes, and asked, "How much did it cost you?"

"I don't know," the man replied, a little nonplussed.

"How come you don't know?" the boy went on. "How can you have a car like that and not know how much it cost?"

"Well, actually, my brother bought it for me," the man answered. "He gave it to me."

The boy was astounded. He was silent for a moment, and then, thinking aloud, he began, "Man, I wish I could — "

Mentally the man finished the sentence for him: *I wish I could have a brother like that.*

But the boy spoke out his heart's wish rather differently: "I wish I could be a brother like that!"

That sentence changed the man's life. It was a modern miracle of sight restored and of eternal riches found in poverty.

How do you feel about this story? When you look back over your prayers, are they about "having" or "being"? Do you think it makes a difference?

Take a look back

Take some time to reflect on where you feel God has been active in your life during, say, the past year. How has this action been fulfilling your desires? Can you see any connections between these desires, to which God has been attending, and the prayers you have been expressing explicitly?

The best gift

I went through a short phase as an adolescent when I longed to have an electric train set. One day just before Christmas, my father came home with a parcel from our local electrical goods shop, and I was thrilled that my dream might be coming true. But on Christmas Day I unwrapped not a train set but an electric blanket!

We lived in a cold, badly insulated house, and the nights came when I was so thankful for a warm bed. But at the moment of unwrapping, I was hardly able to conceal my disappointment. Yet my parents had the longer, wiser view. They knew that my obsession with trains was fleeting, but that my need for warmth would always be there. They gave me what I really needed, not what I wanted.

Look back over some of your life's disappointments. Were they disappointments in the end? Were they good gifts in disguise?

23

Walking with a Friend, Praying with the Church

Companions and community

⁂

*The spiritual world is not universally benign, and
it is possible to lose one's path and flounder. Hence
the importance of solidarity with those who have
trodden the path before us.*

— KENNETH LEECH, *TRUE PRAYER*

The journey into prayer — our journey to God's heart and to our
own — can sometimes seem a very lonely one. At times any and
all of us feel very isolated in our spiritual searching. Perhaps there
are experiences we long to share with another kindred spirit. But
kindred spirits don't just appear anywhere. And when we most
need them, they are often the most elusive.

At times we may feel we are going around in circles or even veer-
ing off course, and we wish we could check things out with another person who knows the reality of the inner journey and takes
our searching seriously. We may even doubt the authenticity of our
own experience, because we know that most of the people around
us would think we had flipped if we were to reveal our prayer.

I suggest that there are two gifts in our lives, waiting to be
claimed, given precisely to hold us on course and to restore our
certainty that we are not amputated limbs but vital cells of a living
body. One is the gift of spiritual companionship with a fellow

believer. The other is the gift of community with the whole body of Christ in his Church.

Anam Cara — Friend of My Journey

Our Christian awareness, especially in the British Isles, has been greatly influenced by the powerful Celtic sense of life as a pilgrimage, and from the Celts we get the term *anam cara,* which means "soul friend." In Celtic Christian communities, a soul friend was a person with whom you could share your journey — someone who would listen, without any judgment, and hold up for you a mirror of your searching so that you would be able to see something of your heart's movement. Together, then, you would be able to discern the ways in which God seemed to be drawing you. Having been invited into your spiritual life, this soul friend might sometimes challenge or confront you for your spiritual good.

Traditionally a Celtic soul friend had no special qualifications, except the one overriding requirement to be a person of prayer, someone who was taking his or her own spiritual life seriously, someone who loved God. Soul friends could be male or female and were frequently laypeople with no status in the Church. It was a ministry in which ordinary believers could accompany one another on the Way. It was also a ministry so highly valued that it was said that "a person without a soul friend is like a body without a head."

The gift of soul friendship, then, is part of our Celtic heritage. And there's good news — that this ministry is increasingly available to us today. The Christian church is reclaiming soul friendship, using any number of terms: *accompanying the journey, spiritual companionship, mentoring,* or *spiritual direction.* This last term, however, is misleading, because a soul friend does *not* direct. God alone, through his Holy Spirit, is the one who guides the pilgrim, and the soul friend simply walks alongside, listening and giving the support of friendship as the pilgrim lives out the promptings of God's call.

How do you find a soul friend? It may seem like a daunting challenge if you embark on it cold. You are, after all, hoping for a companion with whom you can be completely open about your innermost life, someone you can trust completely to hold all that you share in total confidentiality, and someone with whom you feel at ease. The first step is to look, prayerfully, around your own circle of friends and fellow believers. Is there anyone among them who might feel right for this special kind of relationship? Is there someone who is on your wavelength, who has the gift of being able to listen with complete and loving attention, *without imposing her own agenda on you?* This last point is important. The relationship is, in a sense, one-way. The pilgrim shares, and the soul friend listens. Most people find this a most effective way of sharing the journey; anyone ministering to another as a soul friend will also have a soul friend, with whom she shares her journey.

Because so many people find themselves, from time to time, lost and alone on their spiritual journeys, networks of pilgrims have evolved around the country — indeed, around the world — to help individuals find contact with other pilgrims. Generally these networks have sprung out of people's needs for this kind of companionship. They have never been, and never can be, imposed from above, but have grown up from below. They are a potent sign of the desire for growth at the grassroots level, and the need is being addressed at that basic level within believing communities. An increasing number of Christians, both lay and ordained, now seek training in the basic listening skills, enabling them to be alongside others in this way. Almost certainly such prayer guides or companions are living somewhere in your area. In the "Taking It Further" section of this chapter I give an address to which you can write for more details of any such networks in your area.

A relationship with a soul friend will provide the space for the two of you to meet regularly, perhaps every few weeks or so, for you to talk about what seems to have been happening in your relationship with God and in your prayer. You are completely free to say as much or as little as you wish. Your soul friend will know how to be present to your silences and to your tears, as well as to your words and your rejoicing.

Some people explore their life of prayer with a few friends in a faith-sharing group. You may find such a group in your church or neighborhood, or, if there is none, you may feel drawn to start one. I know of one group that meets each Friday morning after taking their young children to school. They gather for an hour in a room in the school and bring a powerful presence of prayer into the life of that school; that's in addition to their giving one another much-needed support in their personal relationships with God.

When we share our journeys, either one-to-one or in a group, we are participating in a special way in what Saint Paul refers to as giving birth to Christ in his world. We are ministering to one another as midwives, tending one another's coming to life and growth, being present to one another's pain, fears, hopes, and dreams, and sharing that moment of wonder when another person recognizes God's presence and holds that new life in his or her arms.

Praying with the Church

We are frequently reminded in our liturgies that we belong to a communion of saints — an invisible body of all believers, those who are living, those who have died, and those still unborn. This is a beautiful and powerful concept, but it can be difficult to get in touch with its truth at a personal level.

It might be helpful to recall memories or impressions of times when you felt in touch with the completeness of God's family in its invisible as well as its visible dimension. I think of two incidents from my memory bank that might remind you of something in your experience of being part of a believing community infinitely larger than yourself.

My first flashback takes me to the city of Prague, during the first springtime following the so-called Velvet Revolution of 1989, which freed the Czech Republic from totalitarian control.

It was Good Friday. In the early evening I joined with a trickle of people making their way to the foot of a hill. As we began the steady climb, the trickle became a stream, and other streams joined it from other parts of town, making a human river flowing up the hill in the first public pilgrimage along the Stations of the

Cross since the imposition of the oppressive regime. As we walked
I looked into the faces of these newly liberated people of Prague,
in their jeans and jackets. I read the story of the past fifty years in
their eyes, but I also read the story of two thousand years of
Christian hoping and persisting and believing.

The next evening the crowds gathered again, all over the city,
outside the churches. For fifty years the celebration of the Easter
Vigil had been suppressed. Tonight, however, the paschal fire was
rekindled from the depths of folk memory, a torch handed on to
us all down the years from the first companions of Jesus whose
hearts had been set alight by the direct encounter with his love.
Gradually the dark of the night was transformed as we passed on
the living light to our neighbors, taper by taper. Then we walked
together into the pitch-black church, turning it into a place
streaming with light and joy and overwhelming gratitude for our
freedom. Each one of us was a light bearer who contributed to
the reawakening of the dark church. That night we knew the authentic joy of resurrection, and we knew that we were one in that
joy, not just with one another but with everyone who had ever lit
a candle of faith in a dark place.

My second memory is of a "last supper" meeting with a friend
who was close to death. I sat at his bedside, torn between gratitude and grief, gazing into the face of a man who had become
one of my wisdom figures. Only hours away from his death, he
was fully alert yet deeply at peace. He took my hands and spoke
his blessing, in the words of the medieval English mystic Julian
of Norwich, who had been one of his special spiritual friends and
guides in the communion of saints: "All shall be well. And all shall
be well. And all manner of thing shall be well."

I had heard the words so often that they had diminished into
mere cliché, ringing hollowly through my own experience. But at
that moment I heard them with a new ring of authority. At that
moment I knew that they were true, because I knew that they were
being given to me by someone whose heart was already dwelling
in the place that blessing described.

My friend was standing on the threshold of a communion of
faith, which was still invisible to me, and he passed its blessing on

to me like a fragment of eucharistic bread. He could have added: Take this blessing and absorb it into your heart, for you too are a living cell in the body of Christ.

Moments such as these are pure gift. They have the power to carry our personal prayer straight to the heart of heaven.

To pray with the Church is to be part of this river of faith. We pray with the Church, of course, every time we share in its liturgy, and being aware that this is what we are doing can help us make that prayer a time of power and grace rather than dry obligation or empty ritual.

If your Christian tradition uses a set lectionary, you can in a special way link personal prayer with the prayer of Christians around the world. You can incorporate the daily Scripture readings into your own day, knowing that others are doing the same with those readings. This is an excellent starting place for the imaginative meditation or forms of scriptural prayer that we have explored in earlier chapters.

Some people choose to pray the "divine office," which links them daily to the official prayer of the Church used by all clergy and religious and many laypeople. Be careful, however, not to let this become an achievement course that you feel you have to accomplish every day; it could also crowd out time for simple stillness before the Lord.

Praying with the Church (which includes the invisible communion of all believers, alive on earth or alive in heaven) allows us to slip into the stream of faith-life that flows through history, through every tradition of faith, and through all time and space.

❦ TAKING IT FURTHER ❦

Start a group

Do you have contact with any faith-sharing group? If not, would you like to? Is there such a group in your neighborhood? If not, you might like to think about starting one, by inviting a few friends to meet and share together how they feel about their relationship with God.

To find a local Christian Life Community (faith-sharing group) in the United States, contact:

Christian Life Community
3601 Lindell Blvd.
St. Louis, MO 63108-3393
314-977-7370
http://www.clc-usa.org/

Explore traditions

Try attending a church service in a tradition other than your own and let the not-quite-familiar words and liturgy work on you in a fresh way, reminding you that you are part of a universal Church, infinitely rich in its diversity, yet united in its longing and searching for God.

Remember the others

In the early morning, when the sun is rising, stop for a moment to remember the people to the east of you who have just come to the end of their day. Let them be present in your prayer. Receive from them, in your imagination, the baton of prayer, which you will carry forward, as a member of the universal Church, through the coming hours of light and activity. In the evening, as the light fades, remember the people to the west of you, who are just waking to the new day. In your imagination, pass on the baton of prayer to them, and remember them in your prayers.

24

Keeping a Spiritual Journal

Teach yourself to patchwork

※

*A journal gives the opportunity to pause and move
down rather than out, to discover, clarify, see new
aspects, explore fresh possibilities.*
— FROM KEEPING A SPIRITUAL JOURNAL,
EDWARD ENGLISH, ED.

Why do we keep diaries or make scrapbooks or even take holiday
photographs? Why do we write love letters or seek the depths of true
companionship? Why do we try to capture our "magic moments"?

We like to keep track of things, by recording our daily, weekly
or monthly doings. Over time that gives us a sense that we are
"going somewhere" and not just drifting, even though such purpose is not usually obvious on the daily journey.

We like to look back on the high spots of our lives. This is more
than just nostalgia. Reliving the times of special meaning and joy is
like reentering sacred space in which we felt enlivened. Revisiting
these special times helps us to trust that the signposts from the
past are indicating a true direction for the future.

*We need to pour out the deepest needs, feelings, and longings
of our hearts,* as we might in a love letter or in a conversation with
a loved and trusted friend.

I would suggest that, just as these are natural human instincts
and desires, so too they can serve to motivate us to try out the
possibilities of what I call patchworking.

Do you remember the story of the school principal's patch-work quilt in chapter 7? The children had made and gathered personal, representational "pieces" by which the principal could remember them.

A journal can be a lot like a patchwork quilt. We write down our pieces and collect them over time. Patching life together in this way is far from tedious, although it can require some discipline. It's so easy *not* to make a note of some incident, thought, or snatch of conversation. Yet, when we collect these patches, we are putting together our inner stories. Only when we read over our past days and moments can we see a more whole picture of who we are and where we are going.

Far from being a tedious chore, keeping a journal can be an enjoyable adventure. Let's consider a few metaphors that show the value of a journal.

A Fly on the Canvas

Imagine a fly walking across a painting in the art gallery. It would see a very strange version of the picture. One stretch of the journey might be all red, the next might be all green, and there would appear to be no connection at all between the steps along the way. Until, of course, the fly flew off to perch on the opposite wall and could suddenly see the picture as a whole. Then the "red days" and the "green days" would be seen as integral parts of the story.

When we record the individual steps along our way, they seem to make very little sense. But if we can look back over a month, a year, a generation, we see quite different patterns and meanings. We begin, imperfectly, to see our lives in the way that God sees them perfectly in all their fullness.

Mountains and Molehills

Time and distance help us to distinguish between the real mountains and the molehills. Day to day, it's not always so obvious. Is this seemingly insurmountable obstacle really inconsequential? And is this niggling, persistent irritation something to slough off or is it a warning about a deep and perhaps damaging fault line? Prayerful reflection over time is the key to such discernment, and a journal is helpful for tracking patterns.

Words for the Way

Many people feel that they receive messages in prayer. For some this may be quite dramatic; for others the messages take the form of gentle suggestions from somewhere deep inside them. Two of my personal "words" have been: "Stay close to the spring" and "Don't water the weeds." These messages keep returning to me, and each time they go deeper. Words like these seem to come from God, and they are valuable patches in our quilts.

The Longest Journey

The word *journal* (and *journey*) comes from the French word *jour,* meaning "day." Our story, mapped out in the patches of our quilt, is the record of a journey. It has been said that "the longest journey is the journey from our heads to our hearts," and that is precisely the route of the inner journey. Our patches are snapshots along that journey of risk, discovery, and joy.

Mr. Craik and the Inkblots

Mr. Craik was a schoolteacher in the days when children wrote with real ink and books were meant to stay blot-free. The children in his class made every effort to offer him unblemished homework, but often they failed. Mr. Craik could have pointed out these failings by circling the ugly blots with his red pen and drawing attention to them with a reproachful exclamation mark, as many of his colleagues did. Instead, he turned each sorrowful blot into an "angel" by drawing his own little picture around it—a pretty face, a smiling sun, a dancing flower.

Some of the pages of your journal will be blotted and spoiled. But God will transform them so as to help and encourage you. We can discover God's enhancements to our inkblots as we bravely go back to them at a later time.

Unspoken Conversations

Our records, with all their emotion and apparent lack of connection, can reveal what God is showing us about the oppositions within. When we write down what is happening in our lives and in our prayer, we may find areas of conflict and contradiction. To return to the quilt image, the patches don't always have an easy, neighborly relationship with one another; the discordant colors can show that different parts of our lives are not happily connected.

When this happens, you might let the conflicting elements hold a conversation with each other. This is sometimes called dialoguing, meaning that we allow different and even opposing feelings and impulses to have their say, within the shelter of our prayer. This can lead to a deeper understanding of ourselves and help us identify important elements of our needs and desires. A journal is a good place in which to hold, and record, this kind of inner conversation.

Samuel's New Coat

In the Old Testament story, Hannah gave her little son Samuel up to the service of God in the temple. Then she brought him a new coat every year, to replace the one he had outgrown. God does the same with us, as he watches us growing in our love of him and of our brothers and sisters. Nowhere is this more obvious than when you come to the end of a year's journal or when you sew together a collection of your patches. A new year is beginning, built on the old and looking toward a future of surprises. A new book is a new coat for your internal growth, a space into which you will grow in ways you cannot yet imagine.

Some Classic Examples

There is a rich tradition of journal keeping that we can look to for help and inspiration. Here are just a few examples.

Dietrich Bonhoeffer, *Letters and Papers from Prison*
Berlie Doherty, *Dear Nobody*
Anne Frank, *The Diary of Anne Frank*
Dag Hammarskjöld, *Markings*
Gerard Hughes, S.J., *In Search of a Way*
C. S. Lewis, *A Grief Observed*
Thomas Merton, *The Journals* (five volumes)
Henri Nouwen, *Sabbatical Journey*

And the finest example of all is the Old Testament, which is the journal of the human race and a patchwork quilt sewn together from the dreams and conflicts, the hopes and longings and betrayals, the inkspots and corresponding angels of the whole human family.

❧ TAKING IT FURTHER ❧

Making a start

You might make a start in journaling by noticing some of your own "patches" and capturing them in some form that appeals to you. A journal can be in any form you like, and it can contain whatever you feel like putting in it. The most usual way of keeping a journal is to keep an easily carried notebook with you; simply jot down things that speak to you of your relationship with God and of your inner journey. These might include:

• Notes on what happens for you during times of prayer; anything God seems to be saying to you or asking of you; ways in which you notice how you respond to God and how God responds to you.

- Incidents or even objects that catch your attention. Look (each day) for a special moment or gift so you can make a note of it and then give thanks to God.

- Places where you have felt particularly at ease, close to God, or in tune with your deepest reality. These are sacred spaces. You may like to keep photographs of them and return to them in prayer.

- Any words or messages you see as having something to say about your journey.

- Special insights.

- Highs and lows of your moods and feelings, and why you think they happened.

- Photographs, or just the names, of people who are significant to you. These can remind you of what these people have given to you and act as prompts to remember them in your prayers.

- Significant dreams; if possible, make a note of them immediately on waking and record them just as they were, without trying to make sense of them.

- Notes or quotations from conversations, TV programs, sermons, books, and so forth, that have come to life for you.

- The names of your "angels" or wisdom figures, including any from the distant past. Try choosing the most important to you and holding a prayer conversation with them or writing a letter to them.

- Moments of panic, problems, crises, or life changes; your deepest questions, doubts, fears, areas of pain. Express them freely. In doing so, you are also giving them to God, and when you look back on those times, you may be astounded at how God has responded.

- Moments when God has touched you and when you have felt truly loved, encouraged, and enlivened.

Record everything you notice as having deeper meaning for you, whether it appears to be good or bad. All these moments, incidents, experiences, feelings, and reactions are patches for your quilt. Slow down, relax, replay your day (or week or month) and savor it. Notice its patches and store them up for yourself in whatever way seems right for you, just as Mary stored up her memories of Jesus' childhood and treasured them in her heart.

Here are some practical matters to keep in mind, as you build this habit.

- Don't ever let your patchworking become a burden or a chore. There's no need to make a daily or weekly ritual of it, and there's no need to feel it has to be "properly" written. Jot down whatever is important to you. You are writing only for yourself.

- Date your entries. This can be quite important when you look back, and it can help you make connections and trace the pattern of God's movement in your life.

- Keep your notebook handy. You'll find that it's like a camera you wish you had with you at unexpected moments. Don't let too much time go by before recording an important item; try to do it in the freshness of the moment.

- Try keeping a record of important times in your life, such as holidays, retreats, transitions, even times of illness.

- Let the focus of what you do be not on yourself but on what God is doing in you.

- Be completely honest. You are writing only for yourself and for God. If it helps, write down your thoughts and feelings in the form of letters to God, telling God exactly how things are with you. The privacy of your journal must be safeguarded. If you cannot be sure of this privacy, you might find it necessary to develop shorthand expressions or symbols to express your feelings in a way that only you will understand.

- Read back over your patches at regular intervals and reflect on how you have grown from them. This helps you focus on what God is doing in you, and it also helps to focus your thoughts on what you might want to share with your spiritual director.

25

Learning from Beyond
the Margins

Prayer from the unlikely

※

*There's a magnet that's pulling us, pulling us against
the fence of this world's limits. I have this strange
feeling that we come from the other side of the fence.*
— RICHARD BACH, QUOTED IN *FORGOTTEN AMONG
THE LILIES*, RONALD ROLHEISER

We can see that our spiritual exploration is not a solitary pilgrimage, undertaken in the hope of saving our own souls or merely
knowing ourselves more deeply. We are part of an entire community in pilgrimage. But what about those people who have, apparently, no part in any such community of faith or of prayer? Does
God ask us merely to sympathize with them, to shake the dust of
their unfaith off our sandals and move on to where we, and our
personal spirituality, find resonance and affirmation? I think God
challenges us in less comfortable ways.

I would like to introduce you to three people who have led me,
in prayer and in life, beyond the religious boundaries we have
erected that divide our respectable spirituality from the spiritually
hungry world.

Steve

I had been praying the passage from John 1:35–39, in which Jesus invites two of John's disciples to "come and see" where he lives and what he is about. Suddenly and unexpectedly my journey to "come and see" took on a life of its own.

It was 4 P.M. in the Market Square. A warm, sunny afternoon. I had picked up my daughter from school, and we were walking between the shops when I noticed a man whose sad, childlike face caught my attention. As we passed him, he held out his hand and asked if I had any cigarettes. No. I shook my head and walked on.

We stopped to buy ice cream and sat on a bench in the sun to eat. The minutes passed, and my thoughts were haunted by the sad face of the man I had passed by — and failed. I had to go back to find him.

He had moved on. Eventually I found him sitting at the road-side near a high-rise garage. I crouched down beside him, and we talked for a while. It wasn't easy to understand him through the intoxication and the crying. But I could see the main characters in his drama: an abandoned child; an alcoholic; a server of sentences; a searcher for home.

He told me his name was Steve. I told him mine, Margaret. I got him something to eat from the nearby bakery. He clutched the roll eagerly, and it occurred to me that it had cost me less than our ice cream. I felt suddenly sick about the discrepancy.

"Where do you sleep?" I asked him.

He looked straight into my eyes and stood up unsteadily. "Come and see." Panic shot through me, and I heard the voice of Jesus ringing out the unmistakable challenge.

Inwardly I took a determined step back from Steve as he pointed down to the dark, deserted basement of the garage. Even in his alcoholic haze — perhaps because of it — he sensed my hesitation. "You're afraid, aren't you?"

I was silent for a few moments. My mind searched feverishly for appropriate excuses and tried to suppress the rising realization that I didn't really want to know where he slept, that I had been merely making conversation.

He urged me again to "come and see." I thought of Jesus. I remembered that at four in the afternoon he too had been entertaining unexpected guests and answering thoughtless questions. I followed Steve down to his home, which was a mattress on the concrete floor in a dark, stinking corner.

We stayed there for a few minutes together, while Steve ate his little meal and showed me his kingdom. His tears flowed and his nose ran. As he took the handkerchief I gave him, his penetrating blue eyes met mine, and I knew that I had discovered where Jesus lives. There was no need to search my imagination. The reality was here at my feet, on a moldy mattress with an empty bottle.

Maggie Martin's Christmas Tree

I had never really noticed the artificial Christmas tree in the rectory, even though the priest (let's call him Mark) whose tree it was, had lived there for nine years. But I did notice it this year, at the time of the children's Christmas Mass, in the corner of the room.

The next day, talking with Mark, I learned about the origins of the tree, which I've come to think of as Maggie Martin's tree. Mark had come upon Maggie Martin when he was working in a poverty-torn parish in London. She had called him in the wee hours of one night, and he had responded to her cry for help by getting up, getting dressed, and trudging out, equipped with the means to administer the last rites if necessary, only to find her the worse for wine and even more the worse for loneliness. It was the first of many such encounters.

Maggie was well in her mid-forties. She had been married and divorced three times, after which she had dispensed with the formalities. "I'd come to confession, Father," she would say, "but I know that if a man knocked at the door I'd be in bed with him as soon as wink." She knew prison from the inside, but the comforts of the Church she could only gaze at from the outside. When the rectory was burgled, however, her faith was absolute: "It wasn't one of the lads, Father. I've told them not to touch the rectory."

One December she had a fight with her lover. Things got rough and feelings ran high. She threw him out into the street and the Christmas tree—his gift to her—out with him. The rejected lover slunk off into the night. As for the tree, she didn't want it back. That would be like taking the lover back. But it was a shame to waste it. She knocked on the rectory door and gave Mark the tree, along with its decorations and an honest account of how she had come to part with it.

Christmas Eve came, and the tree, lovingly decorated, stood in the rectory hall. Mark called on its previous owner and invited her to come and see how beautiful it looked. She admired it, content that in some accidental sort of way the right thing had been done. But honesty compelled confession: "I ought to warn you, Father: They're all stolen, the decorations."

Little by little, the great divide between Maggie's world and Mark's shrank. She started to respect the man who was respecting her. They recognized the Christ in each other and acknowledged between them a part in bringing him to birth. Maggie started to bring herself, her despair, and her hope to Mass. Mark, in return, invited her to try a different, more sustaining kind of wine.

Maggie died of cancer when she was fifty. Before she died she wrote these words to Mark, who, like the Lord he follows, had the grace and the courage to cross over to the world beyond the boundaries.

> I came late to the faith
> A stranger, searching
> from sorrow seeking
> solace, where it hid;
> an outsider, face pressed
> against the window
> looking in . . .
>
> And it seemed that
> I was bade,
> "Enter, and be still."
> And in the celebration

of the blessed bread and wine,
I saw a hand of friendship
and I heard:
"In this sweet oasis,
take your fill."

Whenever I read these words, I think of how Mark has lovingly set up that tree year after year ever since Maggie first brought it to him — how he has adorned it with its stolen decorations and remembered, as he has done so, a broken, defiant face pressed up against the window, and then a face ravaged by the last stages of cancer, and finally the face that battled and found peace at last.

The tree stands there now, each Christmas, shining in the rectory window, with a kind of death-defying joy and an irrational hopefulness that makes despair and its logic look foolish. The tree stands for itself, but it stands there for Maggie, riddled with sin and full of grace, who had the courage to say yes and bring God to birth in a London slum.

The words of consecration are spoken. Maggie's labor, sin, and sorrow are offered up for us all. A mother rocks her son to and fro in the candle glow, and children and parents respond, "Lord I am not worthy to receive you, but only say the Word . . ."

The Word is made flesh, and dwells among us, full of grace and truth. And we behold his glory, twinkling in stolen lights and flickering in broken hearts.

Adam the Child Killer

I have changed Adam's name and the details of his story, but he was real enough, and he had the courage to appear on a TV documentary called "Killing in Common." The program was a series of interviews with people who, for many different reasons, had taken another human life. Some had been responsible for a fatal accident; others had been involved in more deliberate actions. Adam had killed his own child, intentionally.

Adam and his wife, Grace (I have chosen their names with care), had longed for a child. When she was born, it became clear that she was disastrously damaged, both mentally and physically. Her parents and doctors considered the situation and discussed all the possibilities. They came to the conclusion that it would not be right to keep the baby artificially alive indefinitely, but that they would provide her merely with warmth and ventilation and let her die naturally. This process, they believed, would take only a day or two, and she would slip away from them painlessly.

Three agonizing weeks later, the baby was still alive, and her parents were still keeping vigil at the bedside. Then came the moment when Adam's heart snapped open, and his endurance was at an end. For a few moments he was alone with his daughter. He quickly disconnected the ventilator. Almost immediately the baby's heart monitor registered alarm, and the nurse came rushing in. She recognized the baby's terminal distress and its cause and picked her up out of the crib. Then she looked into Adam's eyes, and her heart melted. "Would you like to hold her?" she asked him. "I would," he said, as he took the little girl into his arms, where she died a few moments later.

Adam was interviewed for the program and asked how he had felt at that moment. He admitted frankly that he had no belief in God or in an afterlife and was in no way a religious man, but, he went on, "At that moment I knew a power of love that I had never ever known before. I loved her totally, even as I took her life." His voice faltered as he spoke, there before the cameras, and his eyes filled with tears. He had discovered peace in that moment where love and grief had embraced.

As I watched this program, words of a hymn floated back to me: "Did e'er such love and sorrow meet, or thorns compose so rich a crown?" Adam probably never knew the hymn, but he shared something of its meaning with all those who witnessed this epiphany of love during that program.

God comes to meet us where we dare not walk ourselves.

The Prophet Margins

The world is teeming with Steves and Maggies and Adams. If your heart has found the way across the causeway that connects your life of prayer with your life in the streets, factories, and housing projects around you, you will know for yourself some of the people who beckon *you* to take your believing beyond the boundaries. How will you respond?

Might it be that some kind of a revolution is called for, not in the longing world, but in *us,* the believers in God and followers of his Way? I have a mental picture of the power of God that could be described, perhaps, as a ball of fire with a thin crust surrounding it. The power breaks through that crust at the points where the crust is weakest. I know that I can say, with conviction, that this power has become effective in my own life at *my* weakest points, and I know too that those who have ministered to my spiritual development most effectively have done so out of their own experience of brokenness and vulnerability.

This aspect of God's power — a power that is revealed where we are most vulnerable — might cause us to reflect very carefully and prayerfully on how we are called to respond to people who live beyond the boundaries. We might discover that we are not bringing the gospel to them as much as they are bringing it to us. God's power was seen at its most invincible when his own Son hung, a mangled corpse, in a place of execution. And that Son himself told us to seek and find him among the outcast and the downcast. At the weakest points in the thin crust of our society, he told us, the power of love would be able to break through to us most authentically.

Far from being the unconverted whom we must pull back into the fold of the Church on our own terms and conditions, these people on the margins are prophets of God's power, the first places where that power breaks through into the life of the world, if only we will open our eyes and ears to perceive it. We have more to learn from these people, by far, than they will learn from us. But to learn we must listen, and to come close enough to listen, we must have the courage to step across those boundaries. If we don't know how to do this, we have One who teaches us by his example. An excellent way of getting in touch with this example is to pray the Gospels imaginatively, as suggested in chapter 13. Then we must take what we have learned in prayer out into the world.

Full Circle

And so prayer encircles our hearts in a loving awareness, which includes every one of our relationships. We may seek prayer at first in the hope of deepening our relationship with God and of knowing ourselves more fully. But the circle will be completed only when the whole of creation discovers what it means to be fully alive.

In prayer our human hearts encounter God's heart. Just as our hearts provide the pulse that gives life and continuance to our bodies, so the heart of our prayer gives life and meaning to us and the world. Every time we return from prayer back to the life that lies both within and beyond the boundaries, we are reenacting the Incarnation. We are doing what Jesus did, entering the sweat and blood and tears of life even though it might be so much more appealing to stay in the ivory tower of prayer. We are carrying God's love back to the world that so badly needs it. This is prayer. Sometimes it is uncomfortable, but it is God's way of loving the world through our individual experiences.

❈ TAKING IT FURTHER ❈

Buying fish

I met God while shopping for fish one Friday morning. As I was making my purchase, I saw a sweet and smiling elderly lady selecting a trout. She seemed the epitome of all that is wholesome and good-natured in a human community.

I had to suppress my laughter, though, when she gazed trustfully at the merchant and said, "Please, will you decapitate it for me? I don't like the way it looks at me!"

It was one of those incidents that lighten the heaviness of the everyday, and I might have left it at that, except that I suddenly connected her comment to Herod ordering the beheading of John the Baptist. Perhaps that decapitation was for no better reason than that someone — Herod, his wife, his niece — didn't like the way the Baptist looked at him or her.

So there I was, suddenly at God's side in the marketplace, facing some questions:

- Have you ever tried to do that — to get rid of a person who was bearing some kind of reproach against you that you preferred not to look at? You may not have gone as far as beheading, but what about all those other ways of destroying a person?

- Have you ever avoided someone who made you uncomfortable? Have you walked past a Steve or despised a Maggie Martin or condemned an Adam?

- Have you found ways to eliminate or avoid what needs to be corrected in your life, rather than having the courage to look at it honestly? Is this habit becoming a way of life?

Some weeks after the encounter at the fish market, the daily reading (Luke 9:7 – 9) brought me up against Herod again. This time he was pondering who this Jesus who was causing such a stir might be, and wondering uneasily whether the popular rumors might be true that this was John the Baptist, risen from the dead. "John? I beheaded him. So who is this that I hear such reports about?" reads verse 9.

Isn't it true that whatever we behead keeps coming back at us, in one form or another, until we're forced to see it honestly, to become humble and pay attention?

Still, I hope that dear lady enjoyed her trout!

Who lives out there?

Reflect on anyone you know who is beyond the boundaries — alienated from the church or from society or marginalized in some way. What can you learn from this person? How might you enter a more creative and mutually respectful relationship with him or her?

ADDITIONAL READING

Good Friday People, by Sheila Cassidy (London: Darton, Longman, & Todd, 1991).

26

Letting Prayer Become a Way of Life

Prayer unceasing?

※

*What may have started as a journey of self-discovery
becomes a journey into the great web of connection.*
— MARGARET GUENTHER, *HOLY LISTENING*

We have come to the end of this book about the heart's search for prayer, but I hope that we have actually come to the end of the *beginning*. And if the reflections here have been, in any sense, a jumping-off point into ways of prayer you may not have tried before, where would you like to go from here?

Some of these approaches to prayer may not attract you; others may stir you to further, personal discovery. Whatever the case, pay attention to your heart. Be willing to keep exploring, to stay on this pilgrimage through whatever approach you find helpful.

The Music Box

As we plod on with our daily lives, it's easy to lose sight of what treasure we can discover in our own hearts when we connect them to God's heart in prayer. I remember feeling very much like this one year at the end of a retreat, wondering how I could hope to keep the joy of prayer alive through the "drudgery" of common days.

Perhaps God was reading my thoughts, because when I went into the chapel for the final Eucharist, I was delighted and surprised to hear some unusual music.

For the first time in eight days, I arrived in the chapel five minutes early. It felt good to be able to take my place quietly and collect myself and listen to the music. Usually it was something meditative, a Taizé chant perhaps, but today it surprised me. The delicate tinkling tune of a music box emerged, and it captured my imagination. It almost set my feet tapping, filling me with a light joy.

I listened attentively, and I felt as if the Lord were sitting next to me, leaning toward me rather impishly and whispering: "See! *You* play a tune."

I saw my life then, an old music box, with me turning the crank day after day after day. Most of the time this cranking seems completely pointless. It gets me nowhere fast. It makes my arm ache and my heart ache. It makes me feel used and useless, boring and bored. But into all of my musing, God's whisper broke through: "See! *You* play a tune."

I listened again to the tinkling melody. I *do* play a tune. My endless, daily grinding away is somehow connected to the melody. Before this music box prelude ended and the service began, I allowed myself to hear the larger composition. The little tune took me to the gorse-covered hillside, and the seedpods, exploding with life in the summer sun, added their own sound. The wind joined in, and a storm-tossed raven swooped into the chorus. The river sang the descant as it wound its way down to the estuary, and the sweeping constellations of the black nights provided the full supporting orchestra. It was an amazing hallelujah chorus. And my tune was in there too, my little tune that I crank out day after day.

Something similar came alive for me one bleak, gray day in the ruined nave of Coventry Cathedral, which was destroyed by bombing in World War II. In the reconstructed bell tower, the bell ringers were ringing out the call to evensong. I watched the movements of the ringers through the glass walls of their ringers' platform.

To my untutored eye, it seemed each of them was simply heaving one thick rope up and down, yet the result was a magnificent peal that resounded across the city. Sometimes such a peal was a call to prayer and praise, as it was that evening. Sometimes it was an overflowing of celebration or the steady, inevitable tolling of grief. Perhaps it rang out here in terror as the bombs rained down in 1940. Perhaps it pealed in broken thankfulness when Germany surrendered in 1945 or in the surge of new birth in 1962 when the Cathedral was rededicated.

Prayer — and life! — can be labored, apparently meaningless, often full of dry repetition. The rope hurts our hands. Can there be any connection between this labor and the universal chord? I believe there is.

Praying Continuously?

It's easy, and very natural, to come away from an exploration such as ours here full of enthusiasm and determination to keep going. We probably all know from past experience that this period of enthusiasm can be short-lived. Yet, as Saint Paul tells us, we are called into a lasting — an *everlasting* — relationship with the Lord in which we are to pray at all times.

I used to think that Paul must have been living on a different planet when he urged the Ephesians and the Thessalonians to pray continually (Ephesians 6:18; 1 Thessalonians 5:18). Then one day a friend told me a story about something that had happened to him. He had been walking past a bird sanctuary. Having plenty of time to spare, he decided to spend a few hours there in the peace and quiet of an observation hideout, where he could relax and "bird-watch." He made his way to the hideout and, before he had even reached it, a stranger approached him and drew his attention to the distant call of a bittern, a bird rarely seen on these islands.

I was very impressed and told a colleague about the incident. Now my colleague is, one might say, a *real* bird-watcher, not just a visitor who spends an afternoon in the forest preserve. He takes his hobby seriously. Family holidays mean tents and binoculars, whatever the weather! Anyway, as I was telling him about my friend's encounter with the bittern, he interrupted me. "No, it's not like that. You don't go into the hideout and then start listening.

You listen all the time, and some of the listening may happen to be done from inside the hideout."

"If you are really interested in the world of birds," he continued, "you gradually become *permanently* tuned in to the birdsong. You start to notice every change of tone and pitch and to understand its meaning. More than that, you notice the absence of certain notes or certain birds even. You notice patterns and subtle changes in the orchestration. What you hear starts to make you aware of a whole landscape of life that is totally other than your own yet totally connected." This description of bird-watching sounded more and more like prayer. I thought of how prayer tunes us in to the kingdom of God, to which we are connected, but which is still totally "other" to us in our fallen state.

That night I lay in bed thinking over what I had heard. I thought back over the day I had just lived. From my first waking moments, God had been singing me his signals, in the people I had met, the things I had experienced, the environment I had dwelled in. It was God who held it all together, and there was nothing in my day that was not capable of revealing to me some aspect of its Creator — if only I could learn to listen! When I looked at it this way, my own efforts seemed to get in the way. My determination to pray properly was actually disturbing the very stillness that would make space for the birdsong.

How Hard Should We Try?

There *is* a place for effort. We need to spend time, as it were, in the hideout, to train our inner ears to hear the fullness of God's voice. We do need to practice stilling ourselves and focusing our hearts on God and on his Word in very deliberate ways, such as the exercises we have explored in this book. But the greater reality of prayer is to be in touch with the world that the birdsong reveals, to be in tune with God in every moment of our lives and to find him in everything and everyone around us. And in time we will become increasingly still, whatever we are doing at the time. We will start to hear God all the time.

It is this desire, I believe, that will keep us going. If our pilgrimage depends on our self-discipline and determination, it will probably founder and fail. But if it is fueled by our desire to be close to God, then it has every chance of growing in depth and joy and bringing us daily closer to our home in the Lord. It will become like a plant with a deep root that doesn't depend on the passing weather to stay alive but draws its nourishment from the groundwater, which never fails.

And so I invite you to look at prayer, and your own desire for prayer, through the eyes of my bird-watcher colleague. Let your prayer be drawn gently forward by your desire and not driven by your sense of duty. "Pray as you can, and not as you can't" is sound advice. Choose the ways of prayer that help *you* draw close to God. Be realistic about how long you can spend "in the hideout" (in deliberate prayer) each day, and try to find that time if you possibly can. Far better to make a space of ten minutes for God and keep to it than to try to meditate for an hour at a stretch and then feel guilty because it doesn't work out as you had hoped. I would go so far as to say that guilt of this kind *has no place in prayer.* All such guilt accomplishes is to sap your energy and diminish the quality of your relationship with God. So let it go, and good riddance to it! Let God liberate you from such false guilt.

And when you think that your time in the hideout is over, remember that when you leave (that is, when you are not actually in prayer in any recognizable way), you are working out your daily life in the wide world, open to the song of God in every moment and in every interaction with his people and his world. Like the music box, the daily grind of your life is producing its own constant music that perhaps only others can hear. This, I believe, is what it means to pray continually. The prayer that looks back over the events of the day, seeking God's touch in all that has happened, is probably the most effective key to this continual awareness of God and alertness to his guiding. As I've said before, another great help in keeping your friendship with God alive and well is to talk about your experience regularly with a trusted friend or with a small group of people with whom you feel comfortable.

Flowers of the Night

Speaking of the darkness before the dawn makes me think of the flowers of the night, which open their petals as dusk falls and attract the pollinating moths by means of scent rather than sight.

We live our daylight lives, busy or bored, active or incapacitated, in a world of visibility. In prayer we move into a still, silent, and dark place. Prayer, I am convinced, releases a fragrance within us, though we never realize it, which in turn has the power to attract others to its source in God.

When I come home from work and greet my cat, I know exactly where he has been by the scent of his fur. I know at once whether he has spent the day in the newly fertilized field or in the pile of freshly laundered clothes. He takes on the scent of wherever he has spent his time, and he carries that scent with him around the house. I think we do the same but in less obvious ways. We take on the scent of whatever we choose to be close to. If our hearts live mainly with what is negative, self-focused, or destructive, this will infuse us with the smell of such things. But every minute we spend in prayer, consciously close to God, will soak us in God's fragrance. We will never know that this has happened, but others will! They will catch the scent of God on our lives and be attracted to it.

Faith, perhaps, is this: a joy caught from closeness to God and carried into a hurting world. We catch this joy in prayer, whatever form prayer takes, and we carry it, unaware, to others.

And so I pray for God's blessing upon your heart's encounter with him in prayer. I pray for the light, warmth, and fragrance of God's grace and God's love upon your dawn.